Mastering Mountain Bike Skills

Brian Lopes
Lee McCormack

Human Kinetics

Library of Congress Cataloging-in-Publication Data

Lopes, Brian.
  Mastering mountain bike skills / Brian Lopes, Lee McCormack.
    p. cm.
  Includes index.
  ISBN 0-7360-5624-6 (soft cover)
  1. All terrain cycling--Training. I. McCormack, Lee. II. Title.
  GV1056.L66 2005
  792.6'3--dc22

                                            2004020136

ISBN: 0-7360-5624-6

Acquisitions Editor: Ed McNeely; **Developmental Editor:** Leigh Keylock; **Copyeditor:** Anne Rogers; **Proofreader:** Coree Clark; **Indexer:** Betty Frizzéll; **Graphic Designer:** Robert Reuther; **Graphic Artist:** Sandra Meier; **Photo Manager:** Dan Wendt; **Cover Designer:** Keith Blomberg; **Photographer (cover):** Scott Clark; **Photographer (interior):** Lee McCormack, unless otherwise noted; **Art Manager:** Kareema McLendon; **Illustrator:** Lee McCormack

Human Kinetics books are available at special discounts for bulk purchase. Special editions or book excerpts can also be created to specification. For details, contact the Special Sales Manager at Human Kinetics.

Printed in China   10 9   8   7   6   5   4   3   2   1

Human Kinetics
Web site: www.HumanKinetics.com

United States: Human Kinetics
P.O. Box 5076
Champaign, IL 61825-5076
800-747-4457
e-mail: humank@hkusa.com

Canada: Human Kinetics
475 Devonshire Road Unit 100
Windsor, ON N8Y 2L5
800-465-7301 (in Canada only)
e-mail: orders@hkcanada.com

Europe: Human Kinetics
107 Bradford Road
Stanningley
Leeds LS28 6AT, United Kingdom
+44 (0) 113 255 5665
e-mail: hk@hkeurope.com

Australia: Human Kinetics
57A Price Avenue
Lower Mitcham, South Australia 5062
08 8277 1555
e-mail: liaw@hkaustralia.com

New Zealand: Human Kinetics
Division of Sports Distributors NZ Ltd.
P.O. Box 300 226 Albany
North Shore City
Auckland
0064 9 448 1207
e-mail: blairc@hknewz.com

Mastering Mountain Bike Skills

Contents

Preface

I first met Brian Lopes in a weightlifting class more than 12 years ago. The guy only weighed about 150 pounds, but he set records in almost every lift* in most of the weight classes. I remember him squatting something like 400 pounds: a lean figure, knees wrapped, bar bending. It was obvious this guy was unnaturally strong and extremely competitive.

Brian mentioned he rode bikes a bit, and we decided to ride together. I'd been riding for a couple years, and I thought I was pretty studly on my day-glow pink Diamondback mountain bike. B.L. showed up on a 20-inch BMX bike. He zoomed down a road, jumped from a speed bump to a sidewalk, hopped a curb, zipped up a dirt embankment, and popped into a flat tabletop. I was like, "whoa," and tried to follow. KA-BAAM! My rear wheel imploded, and my ride ended.

It turned out Brian was an AA Pro BMX racer, which certainly explained some things. Soon after our first adventure, he won a mountain bike at a race, and we started riding together. We were so passionate about riding we would ride anywhere, anytime. We did midnight parking-garage sprints. We rode in the snow (it was so cold B.L. jumped into a running Explorer). And we hopped in at the weekly criterium. I got spit out early; B.L. pulled at the front.

I left southern California to get rich and famous, and Lopes moved right to the top of professional mountain bike racing. As it turned out, I toiled in obscurity, and it was Lopes who got rich and famous. We each kept our passion for riding, and we pursued bike excellence on our own separate paths.

One thing I learned is that just because someone can do something doesn't mean they can explain it. Most great riders operate at a level way below conscious thought. They're not worrying about gear choice or pedal pressure or getting hurt. They're just doing. And that's why the typical response when you ask how they did something is, simply, "I dunno. You just kind of do it."

When I became addicted to downhill racing seven years ago, I became obsessed with improving my bike-handling skills. I did a lot of trial and error on my own, and I spent a lot of time chasing better riders. I asked them how they danced through rocks and sailed over jumps, and I heard a lot of that "I dunno" speech. I was frustrated that there was no lesson plan for becoming a great mountain biker. Alpine skiing has a curriculum that systematically leads you from the bunny slope to double black diamonds. Why can't mountain biking?

> **"Few things are impossible to diligence and skill."**
>
> Samuel Johnson (1709-1784). By the way, Johnson raced expert dual slalom, and he was quite the dirt jumper.

> * All but lat pull-downs, in which Brian could not beat me. That still drives him nuts.

For the past few years, I've yearned to create a book to help riders climb the ladder to mountain bike greatness. Meanwhile, Brian has wanted to share his knowledge and experience with the mountain biking world. We have reunited to do just that.

The result is, we're not afraid to say, the most useful mountain biking skills book in existence. This book is unique in several ways.

It's for You

Mastering Mountain Bike Skills is for anyone who wants to ride better, faster, or more confidently. We help you master the skills to ride all kinds of terrain in almost any situation: cross-country, freeriding, downhill, dirt jumping, bikercross, urban terrain, and even skate parks.

It's Thorough

You're holding the most comprehensive collection of modern mountain bike-handling skills in print. It is systematically organized to lead you from core essentials to high-level fun. The chapters give you valuable insight into these skills and more:

- Bike selection and setup
- Balance
- Position
- Pedaling
- Pumping terrain for speed
- Braking
- Cornering
- Wheelies and hops
- Drops
- Jumping
- Speed
- Lines
- Racing

It *Shows* You What to Do

This book demonstrates the core moves with extensive photos and graphics. We dissect every skill and step you through each essential move.

You can read the book cover to cover, or you can flip through until a topic piques your interest. Either way, begin with a skill that's right at or above your comfort level and work on it one move at a time. All you need is a little bit of riding ability and, even more important, the passion to learn. Pretty soon, when people ask you how you pulled an astonishing move, you can tell them exactly how you did it.

Introduction

Practice does not necessarily make perfect. Practice makes permanent. If you ride like a cross between the Cowardly Lion and the Tin Woodsman, you'll make yourself less confident and less fluid. Ask yourself how you want to ride your bike, and then consciously practice the skills that will get you there.

One thing at a time. Whenever you're out riding, concentrate on one skill or component of a skill. Look ahead in the corners, stay low over the jumps, weight your outside pedal, or whatever. Think about executing the move perfectly. Soon you'll be doing it without thought, and then you can move on to the next thing.

Don't let bad habits take over. It's okay to make some mistakes while you're learning. But when you keep making the same mistake, it becomes a bad habit.

Research by Wendy Wood, a psychologist at Texas A&M University, provides some tips for overcoming bad habits. Wood no doubt had smoking and PlayStation in mind, but these tips apply to bad bike habits as well. Let's say that as you do a big double jump, you stare into the gap and abort the mission.

- Make it difficult to continue the bad habit. You could attach a blinder to the mouthpiece of your full-face helmet, so you can't look down. If you tend to grab the brakes for no reason, wrap your fingers around the grips.

- Change your environment. After you stop on the lip a few times, you probably will not go for it. Come back later or try a similar jump elsewhere. When your mind gets caught in a rut, a new situation can shake it free.

- Enjoy the short-term rewards. When you finally get that double or at least take off without staring into the gap, give yourself a Lemon Zest Luna Bar. Yummy.

Think about what you want to do rather than what you're trying to avoid. If you think, "Don't stare into the hole," where do you think you'll stare? Many coaches recommend repeating a positive mantra: "I will fly over there. I will fly over there."

Precision now, speed later. Don't make yourself a human missile and hope you learn something before you explode. When you're working on a new skill, approach it slowly on easy terrain. We want to train effective habits here. Going too fast will introduce errors and greatly increase the danger. Stick this to your refrigerator: Smoothness first. Speed later.

Step Up to a Higher Level

Fun happens where challenge meets skill

When you become a mountain biker, you begin a never-ending journey of self-improvement and good times. You have the most fun when your skills match the current challenge. When you step up your skills, you step up the challenge, and vice versa. Beginners and experts enjoy the same stoke. When you nail your first little double jump, you'll be just as jazzed as Dave Watson was after he sailed 30 feet over the 2003 Tour de France peloton.

As your skills evolve, so does your relationship with terrain. You get more confident and you learn to work a trail the way a surfer works a wave. Although your kung fu changes with the situation (you might be a confident trail rider but a sissy jumper), you probably spend most of your time in one of these three levels.

Level 1: The Trail Works You

Your bike feels new and strange, and you have little faith in your ability to survive a trail. You keep all of your muscles tense, all of the time. You drag your brakes whenever your bike points downhill. You creep slowly over obstacles and frequently stop dead or flop over your handlebars. You don't lean enough in turns, and your constant braking keeps your bike from cornering smoothly.

Riding at Level 1 is herky jerky and, to be honest, not all that fun. You hear experienced riders talk about flow and groove and flying over stuff, but you have no idea what they're talking about. Heck, you might even think they're crazy.

Unfortunately, most people who own mountain bikes never get out of this stage. They either wallow in beginnerdom forever or they just plain give up and stick to the road. If you're in Level 1, don't give up. This isn't what mountain biking is about. The real fun is still to come.

STEP UP FROM LEVEL 1

1. Relax. This is so important, we'll keep beating you over the head with it. If you find yourself tensing up, stop what you're doing and return with a fresh mind. If the tension remains, go work on something that doesn't scare you. Fear and tension make riding unproductive and unfun.

2. Lay off the brakes unless there's a specific reason to slow down. "I'm going really fast right now" is not a valid reason to brake. When it's time to brake, do it like you mean it.

3. Try carrying more speed into rough sections. Get light on your bike to get through more smoothly.

4. Have faith in your bike's ability to roll. That's what bikes do. They roll.

Bad Habit Voids Lee's Clavicle Warranty

After talking with Brian about jumping while writing this book, I started making huge leaps in my jumping ability. I soon nailed the small rhythm sections in my area and felt ready to step up to the speed and distance of a bigger set. Within one session I was working my way through the first, second, third, fourth, and fifth doubles. Stoked!

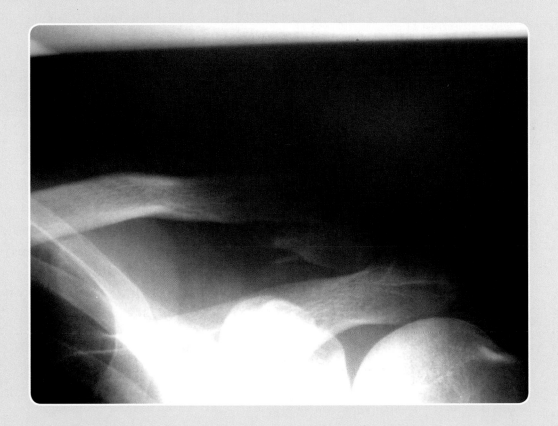

I had one bad habit, though—tapping my front wheel on top of the landing. On small jumps at low speeds, it had never been a big issue. Well, late one evening I was tiring out but decided to do "one last run" so I could nail number six in the big set. On number three, I smacked my front tire right into the face of the landing, fell to flat bottom, and—POW!—broke my right clavicle. Ouch.

The moral of this story: Clean up your technique before you go big. And never take that "one last run."

Brian's Bad Biking Habits

Lee: "Do you have any bad riding habits that you try to overcome?"

(Long pause.)

Brian: "No, none that I can think of."

Level 2: You Survive the Trail

Now mountain biking becomes fun. You've learned to relax a bit. You coast between corners. You roll, clatter, and fly straight over obstacles. In corners you lay off the brakes, lean, and carve like a butcher.

You've become a competent rider. On a smooth, curvy trail you enjoy the sensations of speed and flow. When things get gnarly, you tend to tense up. You bog down in rough terrain and you get bucked out of control when you hit obstacles at speed. You have trouble making corners when traction is iffy.

The majority of satisfied mountain bikers ride happily somewhere in Level 2, blissfully unaware of the next level. When they see pros whiz by with utmost speed and control, they just shake their heads and assume there's voodoo at work. Truth is, severed chicken heads have little (but something) to do with achieving ultimate skill.

STEP UP FROM LEVEL 2

1. Relax. Yes, even more than ever.
2. Commit. The ups and downs of porpoiseful riding require snap.
3. Scrutinize the trail. Not just any line will do. Look for banks to turn on and downslopes to pump.
4. Don't bash into stuff. It's no longer good enough to point your wheel downhill and let it run into whatever's in the way. Instead, try to unweight, wheelie, hop, or jump over the obstacles. When you stop crashing into things, you'll immediately increase your speed and control.
5. Pump backsides. Any time the trail turns downward, press down for some free speed. We're talking any surface here: rocks, stumps, mounds, washing machines, anything.
6. Develop your own style. Experiment to learn what works best for your skills, body type, and equipment. For example, if you can't muscle your bike through rough sections but you rail corners, you might tend to ride around gnarly rocks, which is fine. What isn't fine is thinking you rule at rocks but actually sucking, then bashing into the business end of a boulder. Know yourself.

Level 3: You Work the Trail

This is the ultimate. You ride with relaxed aggression. You never let your front wheel hit a rock, and you never let a backside go by unpumped. The trail is a piece of clay, and you sculpt it to suit your fancy. Your line is as vertical as it is horizontal. You unweight or fly over obstacles, and you press hard into corners. You porpoise through rough sections, gaining speed and control the whole time.

When you reach Level 3, be proud—you're in small company. But just because you can hop a boulder's face and pump its backside doesn't mean you're all that. As you get stronger and better at reading terrain, you'll learn to manipulate trails in even better ways.

Lopes and Peat: Contrasting Styles

Steve Peat and I (Brian) have really different bodies and different riding styles. I'm 5'9" and 165 pounds, and he's 6'4" and 195 pounds.

The taller you are, the more arm and leg travel you have for getting over big obstacles. When Peat reaches a rock garden, he uses his height to move way back and muscle over the rocks. The shorter you are, the lower your center of gravity and the easier it is to corner, so I tend to wiggle around the rocks.

Peat likes to brake very late, enter turns to the inside, and try to carry his speed through the turn. I prefer to slow down before the corner, enter wide, and use my sprint to get back up to speed. When we ride together, Peat tends to drop me entering the corner, but I catch up on the way out.

When we practice a racecourse together, like at the Red Bull Downtown race in the streets of Lisbon, Portugal, one of us tends to be faster in some sections while the other is faster in other sections. At that race, we almost tied in the first run, but Peat won the second run—and 50 100-Euro bills.

Disclaimer

Mountain biking is dangerous. You can break your equipment, and you can hurt yourself. That's what makes it so exciting. Ride within your abilities, and always wear the proper protective gear for the type of riding you're doing. Always wear a helmet and gloves. If you're anyplace you expect to crash, consider elbow and knee pads, body armor, and a full-face helmet. We also suggest eye protection.

The best technique and gear will not prevent all crashes or injuries. If you go out and hurt yourself, it's your own fault. Ride hard and take chances, but don't be an idiot.

Welcome to the exciting, gratifying world of high-level mountain biking. Remember that becoming a great rider is a long-term process. Be patient, take it one step at a time, and have fun! But before you go out and rip, let's make sure your bike is up to the task.

Choose Your Weapon

I f you're reading this book, you're serious about ripping on a mountain bike. (Right on!) Buy a quality bike that matches the type of riding you do, and set it up to match your body and your style. Your bike is an extension of your body—you wouldn't settle for generic arms and legs, would you?

Buy the Right Bike

Aside from your house and your car, your bike is probably your biggest investment. Actually, if you're a hard-core mountain biker, you'll probably spend less on your car than on your bike. So, aside from buying a house, buying a bike is the most important purchase of your life.

Spend as much as you can afford.   Higher-level frames and components work better and last longer than low-end ones. You don't need the ultra-high-end Shimano XTR group to have fun, but it will outlast and outperform XT, just as XT destroys LX, and so on down the line. If you buy a cheap department-store bike, you'll get what you pay for. It will fight your attempts to ride well, and you'll end up soured on the whole experience.

Buy from your local bike shop.   You can find great deals online, especially on accessories, but a local bike shop will help you select the right bike, get you fitted, and keep your rig dialed. If you find a shop with knowledgeable staff and the parts you need, establish a relationship with the staff. You might pay a bit more than you would online, but the experience and convenience will more than make up for the difference. Try bringing your mail-order bike to a shop for a night-before-the-ride repair and see how it goes.

Take it easy on the upgrades.   Don't sweat the components on your bike. Just ride the thing. Here are the most important upgrades:

- Saddle. It's hard to have fun sitting on a plastic anvil.
- Stem and handlebars. They should fit your body and riding style.
- Tires. Choose ones that match your riding conditions.

Run everything else stock until it breaks or wears out.

Hardtail or Full Suspension?

Back in the day, there was no choice because everything was rigid. When suspension forks first came out, downhillers gobbled them up, but the weight weenies stayed rigid in their ways. Now, almost every mountain bike comes with a suspension fork. In the same way, when rear suspension first became available, only downhillers went for it. As the designs got better and lighter, rear suspension appeared on all bikes from the high end on down—for hard-core downhilling and for epic cross-country.

Hardtails are still lighter and cheaper than suspension bikes with the same components, and they can perform better in two particular conditions: (1) cross-country riding on smooth trails and (2) dirt jumping and bikercross on smooth courses. The lighter, stiffer bikes transmit more power to the ground. That's why some racers almost always race on a hardtail.

In almost all other off-road situations, full suspension is superior. You can ride faster and on rougher terrain with more comfort and more control than with a hardtail. Riding is simply more fun—despite a little extra weight and, perhaps, a skosh of lost energy. For most mountain bikers, full suspension is the way to go.

Choose the Right Bike for Your Riding Style

There are as many types of bikes as there are types of riding. If you can't collect bikes the way some people collect shoes or golf clubs, then you need to pick one that suits your typical riding style. Every bike manufacturer has a different interpretation of mountain bike categories, but there are some universal types.

Hardtail bikes.   Hardtails cover the entire performance spectrum, from entry-level rides to high-end racing machines. The layout and geometry have been perfected over the years. If you're a smooth-course racerhead, a hardtail is the weapon of choice. If you ride lots of pavement with occasional smooth trails, a hardtail will work for you, too.

Cross-country race bikes.   Do you want to cover off-road miles as fast as possible? With three to four inches of travel, steep angles, and a weight-forward riding position, cross-country race bikes track well on moderate terrain, handle quickly, and pedal like the dickens.

Cross-country trail bikes.   Cross-country trail bikes are hot tickets for all-around trail riding. They climb well and cover distance with maximum comfort and efficiency. Travel ranges are from three to five inches, with four inches becoming the standard. Trail bikes suit XC racer types who want to ride rougher terrain.

All-mountain bikes.   If you're willing to climb a mountain, but only if you get a rad descent, sign up here. Compared with the geometry of trail bikes, all-mountain bikes' slacker geometry and more rearward position provide greater stability in the steep and rough. Travel ranges from four to six inches. All-mountain bikes can handle only light stuntwork, but they excel on cross-country terrain. They work well for downhillers and freeriders who want to ride trails.

Downhill race bikes.   Downhill race bikes want to flow down rough trails. They're perfect for riders who prefer speed rather than violence and jumping to backside rather than landing flat. You can certainly sprint to clear a gap, but think twice before you tackle that 10-mile climb. Burly frames with six or more inches of travel handle speed well and endure a decent pounding, but they won't endure stunts as long as purpose-built freeride bikes.

Freeride bikes.   More travel and greater durability qualify heavy-duty freeride bikes for mega stunts and punishing flat landings. Precise low-speed handling helps you stick to skinnies and nail narrow lines. Travel ranges start at six inches and go up from there. As for climbing . . . ha!

Dirt-jump and slalom hardtails.   Dirt-jump and slalom hardtails—the unruly cousins of XC hardtails—are burlier and slacker, and they have more front travel.

Their go-for-it handling traits make these the bikes of choice for dirt-jump varmints, urban cowboys, and purist bikercross racers.

Slalom suspension bikes.   Slack geometry, three to five inches of travel, and low bottom brackets make slalom suspension bikes corner like they're on rails. You sacrifice some burliness and efficiency over hard-core dirt-jumping hardtails, but the increased traction and error margin serve racers well.

Not sure what to get?   Throw a dart at this chart. Hopefully, you'll hit near the middle, which is perfect. A trail or all-mountain bike with a four- to five-inch travel will climb as well as it needs to, and it'll treat you right on a wide variety of terrain. These bikes are very adaptable. If you want to ride epic, run a long stem and light tires. For a more DH feel, run a short stem and sticky meats. If you're more concerned with climbing and covering distance than ripping descents, go for a trail bike. If you only climb to earn your turns, go for an all-mountain model.

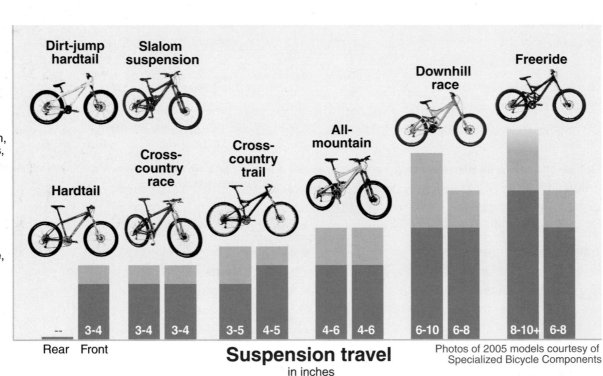

Understanding the Bike's Geometry

Magazine reviews and bike brochures bombard you with all sorts of numbers, but the only number most of us understand is the price. When you buy a bike from a real bicycle company, the angles and dimensions will fit the intended purpose of the bike. Just hop on and ride, and everything will be fine. That said, there are some differences between brands, and many bikes these days are adjustable. So it helps to know how the key specs affect the ride of your bike.

Brian's Quiver

(As of summer 2004)

2004 GT IDXC cross-country trail bike with four inches of front and rear travel. I ride this bike most often because there are more XC trails near me than anything else. I do about half my riding right from my house. The Cleveland National Forest has lots of hard climbs and fast, technical descents. The Luge trail drops right to my street. It has rocks, deep ruts, and rad, bermed turns.

2004 GT Moto slalom hardtail. This is my main jumping and racing bike. I ride it once or twice a week at the BMX track, the dirt jumps, or the slalom spots.

2004 GT IDXC slalom suspension. I've been riding this bike a lot lately because dual slalom is back. There are lots of flat turns, and slalom courses are rougher than biker-crosses because everyone uses the same line. The suspension bike might be one- or two-tenths slower than a hardtail off the start, but it hooks up better throughout a 30-second run.

2004 GT Zaskar cross-country hardtail. I use this for really long climbs and not-too-tough descents, especially if I'm riding with strong climbers I want to hang with. I rode it last week down the Luge, and I got total hand pump. V brakes really suck. You get so used to suspension and discs, it's a trip back in time.

2004 GT Ruckus freeride bike with six inches of travel. I ride this when I don't care how fast I climb and want to have more fun on the descents.

2004 GT DHi downhill bike with nine inches of travel. I rarely ride this bike because it's so hard to shuttle where I live. But watch out, Whistler!

2004 GT road bike. I ride this a few days a week in the off-season.

2004 GT BMX bike. I hardly ever ride this, unless I'm getting ready for a BMX race.

Head Angle

The head angle number has the biggest effect on the way your bike feels. The higher the number, the "steeper" the head angle; the lower the number, the "slacker" or more "raked out" the head angle.

Steep bikes feel nimble. They're easy to steer and easy to keep on track while climbing. On the downside, they feel sketchy on steep descents.

Slack bikes feel stable at speed and on rough terrain. On the downside, they resist turning and once they turn, they like to "flop" to the side. You can feel this in a parking lot. When you veer off line on a climb, a slack bike is harder to correct than a steep bike. You have to muscle a slack bike through slow, tight corners.

Head angle

Lee's Quiver

(As of summer 2004)

2003 Specialized Enduro. An all-mountain bike with five inches of front and rear travel. This is my do-everything trail bike. It's great for XC, light downhill, and even some jumping. If I had to get stuck on a desert island with one bike, this would be it.

2003 Specialized SX slalom suspension. My jumping, slalom, bikercross, goof-off bike.

2004 Specialized Demo 9. Full downhill race bike with eight inches of travel in front and nine in the rear. I ride this guy as much as I can, which is only a couple of days a week maximum, on shuttles, at races, and at ski resorts.

2003 Specialized Allez Pro road bike. About once a week I get out to spin and do intervals.

2003 Specialized P.1 hardtail. One-speed jumping and goof-off machine. This guy helps hone my skills in the winter, plus it saves my pimped-out SX from snow riding.

1995 Specialized Deja Two mountain tandem. My wife and I got "Sheila" as a wedding present nine years ago, and we still rail her on trails. You'd be amazed at the terrain you can ride when you have a six-foot wheelbase and your Smootchie!

Many forks these days allow you to reduce travel (and height) for climbing. A Rock Shox Psylo or Fox Shox Talas fork adjusts on the fly from five inches of travel to about three inches. Dropping your front end by two inches will steepen your head angle by 1.5 to 2 degrees, which makes your bike climb significantly better but descend like a mess if you forget to dial out your travel at the top of the hill.

By the way, an experienced rider can feel a difference of just .25 degrees.

Typical Head Angles

Cross-country	70 to 71 degrees
All-mountain	69 degrees
Slalom, freeride, and downhill	66 to 67 degrees

Our advice on head angle: If you're into steep, gnarly descending, buy a bike with a slack head angle. Dial your fork all the way out or lower your bottom bracket to slacken the head angle even more. With a slack angle, you're dialed for the downhills, and you can manhandle your bike through the tight stuff. A steep angle handles best on flat terrain and is easier to ride overall, but it feels sketchy on the descents.

Bottom-Bracket Height

Your bottom-bracket height determines the amount of ground clearance you have and how high your weight is suspended above the ground. The lower your center of gravity—and your bottom bracket—the better your bike will corner.

Ultra-low bottom brackets like to smash pedals and chainrings onto rocks, logs, and varmints. When you run a low bottom bracket, you have to watch where you pedal.

Long-travel bikes ride high to make clearance for suspension sag and rough terrain. Slalom and bikercross bikes, made for smooth courses, ride low for supreme corner railing.

Bottom-bracket height

Typical Bottom-Bracket Heights

Hardtails	11.5 to 12 inches
Slalom	12 to 13 inches
Cross-country suspension	13 inches
All-mountain	14 inches
Freeride and downhill	14.5 to 16 inches

Our advice on bottom-bracket height: For the best handling, select a bike with the lowest bottom bracket that suits your style. If it's adjustable, run it as low as you can without bashing your pedals all the time.

Random tip: Slow, technical riding rewards high bottom brackets. If chainring clearance is an issue, run a smaller ring or a bash guard.

Chain Stay Length

Short stays are happy stays. They snug the rear wheel under your body for great climbing traction, they make your bike corner more quickly, and they make it easier to loft your front wheel.

Chain stay length

You might be asking yourself, "If short stays rock so hard, why don't all bikes come with short stays?" Well, it's difficult for bike designers to achieve long travel, lots of tire clearance, and the proper chain line with short stays. They usually end up making compromises.

Our advice on stays: Get the bike with the shortest stays that still meets your requirements for tire size and rear travel.

Seat Angle

A steep seat angle, like what you find on a cross-country bike, places you on top of your pedals for optimal pedaling. A slack seat angle moves you back a bit for downhilling. You can still make power, but not as well as you can with a steep seat angle. On most bikes, the seat angle mirrors the head angle to suit the intended type of riding. If your saddle feels like it's too far back, slide it forward on your seat post.

Seat angle

Bike Setup

Since all of our bodies and styles are different, we should adjust our bikes to match. Much of a bike's setup comes down to personal preference, but here are some tips to get you going.

Your braking finger should rest on the end of the lever, and the angle of the lever should match the angle of your wrist.

Controls

Start with your brake levers.

In and out.   If you have good brakes, one finger should do the trick. Most of us use our index fingers, but some crude riders use their middles. Position your lever so that when you reach out you grab the very end of the lever. This gives you max leverage. Pulling the end of the lever versus the middle of the lever can double your braking power.

Tilt.   When you reach for the brakes, your forearm, wrist, hand, and finger should be in line. In general, if you brake moderately on flat terrain (as on a cross-country bike), point your levers downward. If you brake violently on steep terrain (à la downhill), point them forward. Once your brake levers are set up, position your shifters wherever you can easily reach them—and wherever they fit.

Saddle

First of all, get yourself a saddle that feels decent. No bike seat really feels comfortable, but find something that doesn't rub you raw or make you pee your pants. Start with your saddle level and then adjust from there.

Nose down to go up.   For lots of climbing, try pointing the nose down a bit. This concentrates your weight on the blunt rear of the saddle, especially when your bike is pointed uphill. If you plan to climb on a long-travel bike, point the nose down so it doesn't violate you when your rear end sags.

Nose up to go down.   For downhilling, jumping, and the like, try pointing the nose up. When your bike points down a steep slope or starting gate, the saddle ends up pretty level. Also, you can use the front of the saddle for control, but the rear stays out of the way when you need to move back on your bike.

All chain guides have some sort of guide or roller to trap your links on your ring. This guide is made by Gamut USA.

Gearing

For cross-country riding, run what the bike came with. You have 27 gears; surely you can find one that works. (See "Shift Like a Champ" in chapter 3, page 41.)

For downhill and bikercross, run one chainring with a chain guide such as an MRP. For extra ground clearance, tighter ratios, and better shifting, run a smallish front ring (36 to 40 teeth instead of 42 to 46 teeth) and a tight road cluster (11 to 25 teeth instead of a mountain bike's 11 to 34). Give yourself a gear tall enough to go full speed without spinning and low enough to blast out of the starting gate and zip out of the slowest corner. Lower and higher gears are wasted. To guarantee you don't end up in the wrong gear, use your derailleur adjuster screws to block out the ones you don't need.

Tires

Back in the late '80s and early '90s, we all ran Tioga Farmer John or Specialized Ground Control tires. That's all we had, and we ran them everywhere, all the time. Nowadays, mountain biking is hyperspecialized, and there's a tire for every day of the week. While it's strangely fun to take soil samples before each ride and change tires as if they're shoes, you'll get more out of your tires if you pick ones that suit your conditions and run them all the time. Get a feel for how much braking traction your tires have and when they're about to break loose in corners.

Soft rubber compounds improve cornering traction but increase rolling resistance. Some tires get the best of both worlds with soft side knobs and hard center knobs. Thick casings improve durability and reduce pinch flats, but you pay with extra weight. When it comes to compounds and casings, you have to roll whatever suits your situation.

For general conditions—everything from concrete to dirt to rocks to roots to mud—it's hard to beat a tire with sticky rubber and medium, widely spaced knobs. That said, certain situations call for special meat. On hard pack, nothing rolls faster than semislicks—tires with lots of tiny, closely spaced knobs. In sloppy mud, a spike tire grips like male Velcro. You wouldn't want to run these tires everywhere, but in their element they can't be beaten.

The chart on page 10 shows some general tread types. All tire makers have their own interpretations, but most of their tires fit into one of these categories.

Pump it up. The right tire pressure balances speed and traction, cushiness, and pinch flats. Experiment to see what works for you. Start on the high side and let out a bit of air at a time until your tires start to squirm or they pinch flat.

Small and light is good. Some of you freeriders and downhillers love the 2.7- to 3.0-inch tires with thick casings for flat prevention and low pressure for traction. Most people in most situations should run smaller tires with light casings, which accelerate and roll faster. Rely on your tread and compound for traction. To avoid pinch flats, try cleaner lines and smoother riding.

Bar and Stem

Product managers spec bars and stems to match the intended use of the bike and the likely size of the rider. This is a fine starting point, but you might want to customize to suit your riding style.

If climbing is your thing, run a long, low stem—say 90 to 120 mm with 0 to 10 degrees of rise. This creates a powerful pedaling position, and it weights the

Tread style	Advantages	Use	Examples
Semislick with side knobs WTB Nanoraptor	Very fast rolling; decent cornering traction	Very hard-packed trails or racecourses	Maxxis High Roller Semislick, WTB Nanoraptor, Specialized Rockster
Small, closely spaced knobs WTB Mutano Raptor	Fast rolling; good cornering traction	Dry and hard-packed trails	Maxxis Larsen TT, WTB Mutano Raptor, Specialized Roll X
Medium, moderately spaced knobs WTB Moto Raptor	Decent rolling; great all-around traction	All-around terrain from dry to wet. Ramped knobs speed rolling. Grooves in the knobs increase traction.	Maxxis High Roller, Maxxis Minion, WTB Moto Raptor, Specialized Roller Pro
Spike tire with pointy, widely spaced knobs Maxxis Swampthing	Good penetration and mud clearance	Horrific mud and wet grass. Squirmy on any hard surface. For gravity racing only.	Maxxis Swampthing, Maxxis Wet Scream, Michelin Mud, Specialized Evil Twin Slalom, WTB Timberwolf

The 2005 Specialized Stumpjumper Hard-tail is a lean, mean climbing machine. The long stem and low bar stretch you forward for climbing traction and easy breathing.

The 2005 Specialized SX Trail loves gnarly terrain and aggressive riding. The short stem and riser bars settle you rearward for steep terrain and extra-loud body English.

front end for climbing. Run a flat or 1-inch rise bar to keep you nice and stretched out.

If you're more concerned with descending, jumping, and other tomfoolery than ultimate climbing domination, run a 40- to 70-mm stem. This makes it easier to move back for steep terrain, and it gives you a bigger cockpit for controlling your bike. Use a stem with 10 to 15 degrees of rise and/or a bar with 1.5 to 2.5 inches of rise.

When it comes to your bar and stem, long and low works, and short and high works. But long and high feels like you're reaching for help, and short and low feels like you're digging for worms. Not cool.

Everyone prefers a different bar width, depending on their size and the tightness of their forests. Do what feels right, but make sure all of your bikes are the same.

To Clip In or Not to Clip In

There are two kinds of pedals these days: (1) "flat" BMX-style pedals you stand on with soft rubber soles and (2) "clipless" pedals you click into with metal cleats on stiff soles. You young whippersnappers might be wondering why they call the pedals you clip into "clipless." Back in, like, 1492, you slipped your foot into a metal or plastic cage, called a "clip," and cinched your feet to the pedals with a leather strap. These are terrible for off-roading: If you leave the straps loose they barely help you pedal, and if you make the straps tight you're doomed. We used to tighten our straps at the bottom of hills and loosen them at the top, which is pretty clunky—and what if you forget to un-cinch for a gnarly descent?

When the mechanical pedal-and-cleat systems came out, they lacked the big ol' clips, so they were called "clipless." That's like calling a car horseless. Whatever. We will now call these pedals "clip-ins" or "clips."

Flat pedals work best with soft, relatively flat soles. Leave the macho lugs for hiking. This pedal is made by Specialized Bicycle Components.

Clip-in pedals require shoes with holes in their soles to accommodate the metal cleats. When your sole wears out, the cleats make a cool "click, clack" sound on hard floors. This pedal is made by Shimano.

Anyway, clips give you significantly more power than flats. They also improve control, especially on rough terrain—you can float over rough stuff and you don't have to worry about your feet bouncing off the pedals. A few downhillers still insist on running flats, but they're in the minority. You quickly learn how to clip in and out, and in a crash your feet almost always release. *Almost* always.

Flat pedals definitely give you more leeway in certain situations. They're a must for learning to jump and manual, and they make it easier to jettison your bike when North Shore stunts go awry. You can tweak your legs out and lift part of your foot for more balance, and when you take your foot off for corners, you can resume pedaling sooner than with clips.

A lot of people (including the authors, back in the day) feel like they can attack harder and push the limits more with flats. If you're most comfortable with flats, go ahead and run 'em, especially when you're just goofing off. For racing, we suggest you get used to pushing the limits on flats and then switch to clips for their increased power and control.

Suspension

Properly dialed suspension makes your bike ride like a dream. A poorly adjusted suspension setup makes it ride like a nightmare. Properly dialed suspension does two things: It isolates your bike and body from violence and it keeps your tires in contact with the ground.

In the past couple of years, shocks have been getting increasingly complex and tunable. If you're running the latest offering from Fox, Progressive, Answer, Romic, Avalanche, or others, we recommend consulting your owner's manual. But because most shock manuals come from the convoluted minds of suspension engineers, we thought we'd explain the basics. These notions apply to simple forks and shocks with one adjustment each for rebound and compression damping and no fancy-dancy pedaling platforms.

Fork parts

— Steerer

— Crown
— Stanchion
— Arch

— Slider

— Dropout

Shock parts

— Reservoir

— Preload collar

— Coil spring

Spring Rate and Preload

Your spring controls the amount of force it takes to compress your suspension. The higher the spring rate, the stiffer the spring. You fine-tune coil-spring shocks by turning the preload collar. With air shocks, you add or remove air.

You want your spring stiff enough to support your weight but soft enough to sag while you're on your bike. This sag allows your wheels to stay on the ground while you traverse little bumps and dips. The softer your suspension, the more stuck to the ground you'll feel. The stiffer your suspension, the bigger hits you can take without bottoming out. You want your suspension to be as soft as possible without bottoming out all the time. If you use the full travel range a few times per ride, that's perfect.

Most cross-country bikes should sag through about 25 percent of their travel. Longer-travel downhill and freeride bikes should sag about 33 percent. A few designs require up to 40 percent sag. Your bike's manual will tell you what's up.

Put a small zip tie on your fork stanchion and an O-ring on the shaft of your rear air shock. Get on the bike with your weight distributed as if you're riding and see how far your high-tech indicators move in relation to the available stroke. With coil shocks, measure the distance between the shock mounting bolts. Sit on the bike and have someone measure the shock again. The difference is your sag. Of course, it helps to know the total stroke of your shock. If you lost your manual, remove the coil spring and see how far you can compress the shock by hand.

With air shocks, increase or decrease the air pressure until you get the right sag. With coil-spring shocks, tighten or loosen the knurled metal collar on the end of the spring. This changes the preload. If you can't get enough preload with two turns, you need a stiffer spring. Too much preload makes your wheel chatter on small bumps and can damage your shock. If you loosen the collar so much your spring is rattling around on the shock, you need a softer spring.

Rebound Damping

The rebound circuit on your shock slows your spring's extension after you hit a bump. Without rebound damping, your spring would spring back full force and buck you like Buck Rogers—into the 25th century.

If you have too much rebound damping, your shock can't extend after you hit a bump, and as you hit more bumps your shock "packs" lower and lower into its travel, giving you a harsh experience. The faster you go and the more rapid the hits, the faster your rebound must be. If you have too little rebound damping, your bike will bounce—boing, boing—after bumps and drops.

Set your rebound as fast as possible without it feeling springy or hard to control. Also, check your setting every time you change your spring. Your front and rear should rebound at the same speed.

Suspension Setup Tips

✓ Experiment with the extremes. Dial your rebound or compression all the way in or out and see how that feels. Same with your compression.

✓ Change only one thing at a time.

✓ Make notes of your settings and how the bike feels.

✓ Once you get your bike dialed, don't mess around with it too much. Just ride it and get used to it.

Compression Damping

Only higher-end forks and shocks have compression-damping adjustment. Factory settings usually work just fine and, besides, you can mess up your bike's ride with the wrong settings.

Although your spring determines how much force it takes to compress the suspension, your compression damping controls how fast your suspension can compress. Lots of compression damping reduces pedaling bob but can make your bike feel harsh. A low amount of compression damping makes your bike feel plush, but it might bottom out.

For a plush ride, run as little compression damping as you can without blowing through your travel. For efficient pedaling, run as much compression damping as you can without feeling harsh.

Suspension Troubleshooting

Before you mess things up worse, make sure your sag (and, thus, your spring rate) are correct.

Problem: Bike bounces up and down (boing, boing) after hitting a bump or dropping off a curb.

Solution: Increase rebound damping.

Problem: Bike feels good over the first bump but gets harsher over subsequent bumps.

Solution: Your shock is "packing up." Decrease rebound damping.

Suspension Is Getting Smarter

For a few years there, you'd go to your garage (or the bike shop) and choose between a rigid and suspended bike. "Hmm . . . do I want to get up the hills easily or do I want to rail the descents?"

Then came on-the-fly lockout, which let you ride a hardtail up and a dually down. That was great, but we've all struggled down a gnarly descent thinking we were having an off day and then realized we were still locked out. Nowadays, advanced damping systems do the thinking for you. "Pedaling platforms" resist pedal bob but embrace bumps. On rough climbs you pedal like a champ yet track a river. On fast descents you rail like a freight train yet accelerate like a bullet. You don't have to decide which bike to bring or which way to swing the lever; you just ride your bike and have fun.

Problem: Excessive bottoming (even with correct spring rate); too much bouncing while pedaling.

Solution: Increase compression damping.

Problem: Bike feels harsh on big bumps, feels harsh or chatters on small bumps, has poor traction in corners, is not using full travel.

Solution: Decrease compression damping.

A freshly dialed bike is truly a thing to be proud of—the sweet frame, the dialed suspension, the perfectly adjusted controls. But a new bike is merely a thing. It takes a few great rides—a brush with death, a glimpse of greatness, a moment of exultant flow—to bring your steed to life. A perfectly functioning bike becomes more than an assembly of expensive parts. It becomes an individual, a friend, a part of you.

2

Become One With Your Bike

Ride (*v.*): to sit on and be conveyed in a certain direction

When you ride something, you're an inert hunk of cargo. You ride a roller coaster. You ride in a Pinto. If you try to "ride" your bike over a log, you'll soon be a bump on that log. "Ride" is too passive a term for what we do on bikes.

Drive (*v.*): to control, to propel

Driving is active. You drive golf balls. You drive cattle. To truly rip on mountain bikes, you must constantly move and let your bike move beneath you; you must alternately cram your bike into the ground and let it fly unfettered. You seldom sit there and go along for the ride. No, you don't ride your bike—you drive it.

Learn How to Touch Your Bike

Your relationship with your bike is probably one of the most intimate in your life. Your bike gives you pain, it gives you pleasure, it spends the night in your bed. The least you can do is learn how it likes to be touched. You contact your bike in three places, each with its own purpose.

Pedals

These little spinning platforms form the basis of your relationship. When you stand on your pedals, your weight runs through your bottom bracket and spreads about 40/60 to the front and rear wheels. This is where your weight belongs. Here's why:

- Front–rear balance. Your weight stays safely between your wheels, and your front stays just a bit lighter than the rear.
- Low center of gravity. With your weight focused 12 or so inches off the ground, your bike whips easier than a strap of leather.
- Your biggest muscles bear your immense weight . . . ha!
- Your hands stay light on the bars.

Handlebars

Believe it or not, your handlebars are *not* for holding your upper body up. You have a lot to do with your bars—steering, pulling yourself forward, pushing yourself back, pressing down to weight, and pulling up to unweight—so the less you lean on them for basic support, the better. Here's why:

- More comfort. You place less stress on hand nerves and shoulder muscles.
- Better handling. Your bike steers more easily and a light grip allows your front wheel to flop around as it whips into corners and bashes into things.
- More stable. Less weight on the bars makes your bike less likely to pitch you over them.

○ Ready for action. When you lean on the bar, you half-commit in the downward, lazy direction. When you hover over your bar, you're poised to push, pull, steer, lean, or leap over tall buildings.

Saddle

We should all feel close to our saddles, but we shouldn't sit too often or too heavily. Your bike saddle is not a seat—at least not the kind you want to sit on—but it does serve three purposes:

○ A place to rest. When you pedal very hard, all of your weight pushes down on the pedals. This is a good thing, for as long as you can keep it up. Your saddle lets you rest while you pedal softly. The lighter you pedal, the heavier you sit.

○ A platform for efficient pedaling. Even if you aren't sitting with your full weight, your saddle helps smooth your pedal stroke and saves energy you'd otherwise spend holding your body upright. Also, when you push across the top of the stroke, you brace against the rear of the saddle.

○ A point of control. Back in the day, there was a BMX bike with no saddle for maximum lightness, and it was really hard to ride. Even if you don't sit on the seat, you use it to control your bike's side-to-side movement. Sitting back on the seat increases rear traction for climbing and cornering.

When you plant yourself on the saddle, you limit yourself to smooth terrain, mellow cornering, and soft braking. When you cross rough terrain, corner hard, or brake with authority, get up and off that saddle. Even a slight unweight is better than a full sit.

In summary: Stand on your pedals. Use your handlebars for control. Use your saddle sparingly, for rest and control.

Optimize Your Sense of Balance

You zip down a wooded singletrack, and a log appears across the trail. Your inner ears sense downward acceleration. Your skin senses pressure and cold. Your muscles and joints tell you you're crouched on your bike, with your weight planted nicely on your pedals and your bar dancing in your loose grip. Your memory reminds you that if you clip that log at an angle, your tires will slide out and you will crash.

All this information (and more) collides in your brain stem, which sorts it out and fires off the instructions to slow down, approach the log at a right angle, and then hop like a yoked bunny—all in a fraction of a second, without conscious thought.

You perform impressive acts of balance every day—for example, kicking a door open with your arms full of groceries or Rollerblading with your dog on a leash. Heck, you're great at staying upright. If you just relax and trust your innate ability to keep your ass below your teakettle, you'd be amazed at the situations you can drive through. That said, here are some things to keep in mind:

Relax.   Your muscles have to be loose and ready to move.

Stay out of it.   The calculations are way too rapid and complex for conscious thought. If you butt in and try to help, you'll screw everything up. The instant you start thinking, "I better stay upright," it's all over. This is especially difficult any time you're cracking through your skill or fear ceiling. You might track stand without a care in front of Starbuck's, but balancing on a skinny bridge will get your inner mother screaming.

Look where you want to go.   When you look somewhere, you tell your brain and body that's where you want to go. Next time you stare at a scary rock, notice how your head drops and you smash directly into that rock. As they say in every driving and motorcycle-riding program, "Look where you want to go; go where you look."

Practice.   Not only riding, but also balancing. Work on track stands. Practice slow riding. Stand on one foot while you wash your hair. Anything that improves your balance improves your bike riding.

Carry a really long pole everywhere you go.   Especially on tightropes.

Stay on Your Bike

Zones of balance

Imagine yourself running along a trail. You cross ferny flats, climb rooted rises, drop into rutted ravines, and leap spongy stumps. You lean forward when you go up, lean backward when you go down, and lean sideways when you turn. As long as your weight stays between your feet, you stay balanced, and everything is fine.

Staying balanced on your bike is pretty much the same, except your feet are wheels. The better you get at keeping your center of gravity between your wheels, the more time you'll spend smiling on your bike, rather than cartwheeling beside it.

Side note: Side-to-side balance has everything to do with cornering forces. For more about cornering, check out chapter 5.

Flat Ground

On flat ground there's plenty of leeway for you to move forward or back. As long as you focus your weight on the pedals or saddle, you're unlikely to go flying off the front or back of your bike. That said, your bike will brake and corner best if you keep your weight centered. As we said earlier, put your weight on your pedals and keep your hands light on your bars.

Uphill

As your front wheel comes up, you have to move forward. It's all about keeping your weight centered, with enough on your rear wheel to transfer your pedaling power and enough on your front wheel to stay on track.

Sitting: Bend your arms and pull your torso forward. If that isn't enough, scoot forward on your saddle. On really steep climbs, you might be on the very tip of the saddle. Some saddle brands, such as WTB, slope the nose downward so you can perch at the end and not feel too violated. Long stems help position you for climbing.

When climbing in the saddle, settle into the back of the bike for max climbing traction. Pull your upper body forward a bit to keep the front wheel tracking.

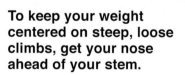

Standing: Pull yourself forward until you're balanced on your pedals. If you're not far enough forward, your front end comes up and your wheel wanders from side to side. If you're too far forward, your rear wheel slides out. Or you spontaneously do a front flip. Whammo!

To keep your weight centered on steep, loose climbs, get your nose ahead of your stem.

Downhill

The steeper it gets, the farther back you need to be. But don't overdo it: Volumes of magazine articles have convinced people to get behind their saddles whenever they descend. This is not only unnecessary, it also makes your bike handle poorly. Your front wheel gets too light, and it dances randomly instead of tracking precisely.

Get way back when it's this steep (about 45 degrees). Watch that front brake; it controls your speed but it wants to pitch you forward.

When you coast down a trail, you should be balanced over the middle of your bike. If the grade is 10 percent, you only need to lean back about 10 degrees. Any farther than that and your front wheel is too light for effective braking and cornering.

On steep descents, lean back with your arms almost straight. Bent arms let your front wheel flop all over the place; straight arms act as a steering damper. If you're not far enough back: The rear wheel wants to lift off the ground, and you feel like you're being pitched forward, which you are. The rear brake skids easily. If you're too far back: With all your weight on the rear end, your front tire will slide and skip in corners. Also, your rear tire will buzz your bum. Which isn't all bad, really.

Pushing the Limits

At 70 degrees, The Manager drop at Whistler is so steep that no matter how far back you get, your center of gravity dangles in front of your front tire's contact patch. Lifting your front wheel helps a bit.

As descents get steeper, your window of balance narrows and, paradoxically, it gets harder to move your weight far enough back. Long stems pull you toward the front of your bike. High saddles get in the way. Your rear tire buzzes your butt. These iffy situations make it more important than ever to:

Lay off the brakes. Here's a paradox for ya: The steeper the trail, the less you should use your brakes. Too much lever pitches your weight even farther forward. Besides, traction sucks on a cliff.

Get as low as you can. This gives more traction to the rear wheel and stabilizes your balance.

When terrain gets extremely steep, there comes a point when balancing on the pedals isn't far back enough. For most bikes this happens when the pitch reaches about 60 degrees. What to do? Get even farther back—and lay off that front brake.

To get a feel for balancing on your pedals, coast down a slight grade and stand on your bike with some weight on your hands. Move your body backward until your hands hover lightly on the bars. If you lean so far back that you have to pull with your hands, you went too far. This light-handed place makes a good base of operations. For cornering, you want more handlebar pressure; for rough terrain, you want less handlebar pressure.

On the Brakes

When you slow down, momentum carries your weight forward. The harder you brake, the farther you must lean back. If you're not back far enough, your rear wheel skids (this could be a case of too much rear brake) or comes off the ground (this is definitely because you're too far forward). If you have dual suspension, your rear end will jack up and your front end will dive. This steepens your head angle and makes your bike very sketchy, just when you need it to be the least sketchy. If you're too far back, your unweighted front wheel skips around like a stone on water. If it locks and suddenly catches traction, *you'll* skip like a stone on water.

When you brake moderately, you can resist the forward push with your arms. The harder you brake, the more important it is that you resist with your legs. When you brake really hard on steep terrain, try to move back, drop your heels, and drive your weight into the pedals. You know you're perfectly balanced when you neither push nor pull on the bars.

Accelerating

No doubt you have a hard time controlling your power. You're forever roosting your friends and tearing up cobbles. Not only that, but your front wheel tends to come up while you accelerate.

Wheelying down a bikercross start ramp won't kill you, but you have to control that power out on the trail. Lean forward while you're on the gas.

Using Your Entire Cockpit

Enjoying a trail—railing turns, hopping logs, and pumping humps—is all about shifting your weight fore and aft, side to side, and up and down. To do this effectively, you must move around. Your cockpit has to give you space to work, and you must be loose and energetic enough to use the space.

Brian's Steepest Descent

I rode this rockslide in the south of France with Anne-Caroline Chausson and Cedric Gracia. It was so steep you didn't want to let go of your brakes or you'd pick up too much speed, but it was so loose you couldn't go slow—your front wheel just plowed—so you went super fast automatically. You could barely steer. I was scared the entire time. I put a foot down, got back behind the seat, and tripoded down so I could lay it over if I needed to (which I didn't).

When you brake this hard, get behind your saddle and drop your heels to brace against your pedals.

Certain situations ask you to get high and forward, or low and back. Don't just sit there—do something!

Explore the limits of your bike's cockpit:

- Pull forward until your tender bits hit your stem.
- Push back until your arms straighten or your bum gets the knobby treatment.
- Lean all the way to the side until your saddle hits your thigh or, with a low saddle, your frame hits your shin.
- Stand so high you can touch the sky.
- Crouch down and look at the bottom of your bottom bracket.
- Do the Hokey Pokey and turn yourself around. That's what it's all about!

The more comfortably you can use your entire cockpit, the better. Move around a lot. Never try to maintain any one position—in turns, while climbing, or whenever. Conditions change constantly, and you have to change with them.

"For every action, there is an equal and opposite reaction."

Newton's third law of motion

Loading and Unloading

Have you ever seen a really smooth mountain bike rider (driver) just floating along a rough trail? He passes over rocks like water over porcelain, bounds over logs like a porpoise over a skiff, and gains speed without even pedaling. He might have a deal with the devil, but chances are he accomplishes these feats by strategically weighting and unweighting his bike.

Try this experiment:

- Stand on a spring-loaded bathroom scale. Let's say you weigh 150 pounds.
- Suddenly crouch down (unload the scale). Depending on how fast you drop, the scale might go down to 50 pounds or even to 0 pounds.
- Pause at the bottom. The scale reads 150 pounds again.
- Stand up quickly (load the scale). Depending on your explosive power, the scale might tip 300 pounds or more.
- Rapidly crouch down then immediately spring back up (preload the scale). By loading your moving mass against the scale, you generate even more force. With good timing, you can hit 400 pounds plus.
- Imagine the scale has a handle attached to it. If you pull upward as you leap upward, you can lift the scale off the ground and read a negative weight. This is a massive unload, like when you hop and jump.

Weighting and unweighting your bike works the same way. When you learn to control the pressure between your bike and the ground, a whole new level of riding opens to you. You can pump terrain, find traction in corners, hop across logs, hover over rocks, and soar over jumps.

Here are the keys to that new world:

Accelerate!   When you fall or rise at a constant speed, you weigh however much you weigh. Sorry. In order to change the scale, you have to gain speed the whole way. Let your body fall unfettered. Drive upward with gusto.

Make the best of it.   These effects last only as long as you can push or pull. You can push hard for an instant or push easy for a moment. It depends on the situation: all at once to hop a hippopotamus or slowly to rail a dusty Martian corner.

Be decisive.   Change direction rapidly. Moves like jumps and hops require rapid, massive loads with sudden releases and drastic unloads. Make it count. You are a Super Ball. Boing!

Time your suspension.   Suspension makes preloading absolutely necessary. When you press down to make a hop, you want your power to drive into the ground, not into a spring and shock. Preload so your suspension is completely compressed when you begin your takeoff. The more travel your bike has, the longer this takes. When you first try a diving board or trampoline, you bounce up and down to get a feel for the amount of flex and then you time your jumps so you sink all the way down and spring all the way up. It's the same on your freeride bike.

Load your suspension as you reach a takeoff. The greater the load, the greater the unload.

Think three-dimensionally.   Once you get the hang of this, two-dimensional riding will no longer suffice. Don't just roll along a flat ribbon. Bounce up, drive down, and throw your weight all around.

Apply it.   Check out the chapters on braking (chapter 4), cornering (chapter 5), hopping (chapter 6), and jumping (chapter 8). When you learn to control your weight, you'll enjoy these skills at an even higher level.

Different States of Weights

Weight	Amount of gravity	Situation	Application
Negative weight	–g's	Pulling your bike away from the ground toward your body	Clearing a rock or jump
Weightless	0 g	Flying, freefall	Hopping, dropping, jumping
Light	0-1 g	Lightening the bike over rough terrain	Skimming over roughness, preparing to preload
Normal	1 g	Sitting or standing	Just riding along
Heavy	>1 g	Pressing the bike into the ground	Gaining traction, pumping backside, loading before a hop or jump

Getting Lighter—Unloading Your Bike

Riders who seem to float over rough terrain are often described as "sucking up" the bumps or riding "light on their bikes," which is exactly the case.

When you sit statically on your bike, the two of you behave like one heavy object. Any time you lift your bike upward or let your body fall toward the bike, you act like two separate objects: (1) your bike, which is light but has to bash into everything, and (2) you, who are not so light and would rather not bash into anything. The faster you lift your bike, the lighter it gets. Here are some uses for temporary lightness:

A little lighter—suck up a bump.   You zoom down a fire road, and a three-foot-tall water bar appears in your path. When you hit it, relax your arms and legs and let your bike push up into you. If you and your suspension suck up two feet of the bump, your body only rises one foot.

A lot lighter—absorb a shock.   As you cruise along a nice little trail, you encounter a six-inch root. When your front wheel hits the front of the root, bend your arms to let the bars come up toward you and then let the wheel roll down the back of the root. When your rear wheel hits the root, relax your legs to let the bike roll over, then straighten on the backside. Your lightened bike will buck up and over the root, but your body will carry smoothly down the trail.

Ultimate lightness—pick up over an obstacle.   You're hauling the mail down a race course, and an 18-inch rock squats in your path. Preload your bike into the ground and then, as you reach the rock, hop your bike sharply upward. This will unweight the bike so much, it'll come off the ground.

Getting Heavier—Loading Your Bike

Although most of the people in the United States are too heavy and want to be lighter, mountain bikers, who tend to be light, should try to make themselves heavier—at least sometimes. The harder you press into the ground, the heavier you get. This is an awkward time to bash into a rock, but there are some wonderful uses for this temporary heaviness. Here are some of them:

Press down—pump terrain. You've unloaded up the face of a water bar, and you crest with your bike sucked up into your body. When you reach the backside, press your bike down into the ground until you're standing straight. The down slope will convert some of this down force into forward speed. Cool, eh?

Drop and stop—brake harder. You're zooming down a hill, and you need to brake really hard to make a corner. Just before it's time to brake, stand up. Drop your body toward your bike and, at the instant you reach bottom, hit the brakes. The extra down force yields extra traction love.

Drop, stop, and press—generate traction. You're tooling along a dirt road, and a tight corner seems too slick for your speed. As you approach the corner, drop your weight toward your bike. All at once, as you begin your turn, stop your fall and push yourself back up. This loads your tires into the ground and gives you mega traction.

Preload your bike—catch some air. To hop over a huge log, you need more up force than you can muster from a static crouch. Approach the log standing up. Drop your body toward your bike. This creates downward momentum. As soon as you reach bottom, explosively push yourself back up. Your downward momentum combines with your downward push and you get a huge upward surge. The faster you drop and the more suddenly you push back up, the bigger your hop.

Mounting and Dismounting

Getting on and off your bike might seem like the most basic of skills, which they are, but the faster you can get to your feet, get past an obstacle, and get back onto the pedals, the better. Nobody carries their bikes faster than cyclocross racers. Practice these moves, and soon you'll cross the unrideable (and recover from crashes) with your speed (and pride) intact.

ROLLING DISMOUNT

1. Unclip your right foot and swing it behind your bike. Always dismount to the left, to avoid those nasty rookie marks from your chain.

2. Swing your right foot forward between your left foot and the bike.

3. As you set your right foot onto the ground, unclip your left foot and hit the ground running, right foot first.

Practice doing this at higher and higher speeds. You'll be amazed at how fast you can do this. Soon you'll bound over inflatable alligators with no loss of speed.

RUNNING MOUNT

1. Run alongside your bike and thrust yourself upward with your left leg. While you're in the air, swing your right leg over the saddle.

2. Land on your right inner thigh. We don't have to tell you to be careful, do we?

3. Find your right pedal and push down. Catch your left pedal as it crosses the top of your stroke, then get out of there!

Try to land on your saddle with your feet already on the pedals. When you master the cyclocross mount, the tough thing will be resisting the urge to wear knickers and a wool jersey.

Crashing

Crashing happens, and it usually happens fast. You rarely have time to think, "Uh oh, I better tuck my arms in. Okay, now I better roll. . . ." It's more like—smash!—and however you're programmed to react, that's what you do. So our advice: Learn to fall correctly as young as possible. Go to Gymboree and master tumbling before you become a six-year-old BMX ripper.

Okay, too late. Here are some notions to consider next time you're hurtling toward devastation.

Roll with it.   Do not try to stop your fall with your arms, legs, or head. They will break. Hit the ground loosely, and then roll with it. That said, some crashes are so violent that bones break before muscles can react. Wear your pads.

When you're surrounded by air, abort the mission.   When you have a bad takeoff, you'll know it as soon as you leave the lip. If you can't correct it right away, bail and try to land on your feet.

When you're surrounded by gnarl, ride it out.   You'll be amazed at what you can drive through. Do whatever you can to avoid stepping into rocks, ledges, and other gnarlies. If you know you're destined for disaster, steer into soft bushes.

Nothing gets your heart pumping like a great save. It's happened to all of us. You hit a jump wrong, get bucked into an endo, and dead sailor through the air, just holding on, and somehow you pull it off. It's like, "Oh my God, thank you," then "Yeah! That was so rad!"

Shoot Your Troubles

Problem: Your shoulders or triceps get tired while you ride, even when you aren't doing gnarly stuff. Sometimes they get tired while you climb.

Solutions: You're slumping and putting too much weight on your bars. Sit up straighter and put more pressure into the pedals. Also, your bike size and stem length could be wrong. Visit a quality shop for a fit.

Problem: On steep climbs, your front tire wanders around like a balloon on a windy day.

Solution: Your weight is too far back. Crouch low and forward with your head and shoulders up past your handlebar.

Problem: As you descend rough terrain, your rear wheel tends to bounce upward and you feel like you're getting bucked over the bars (heck, you might actually go flying over those tubular babies). It's amazing how many people blame their bikes for this problem. ("Dude, my old bike totally flipped me over the bars. This bike is way better.") But this fiasco is due mostly to poor balance.

Solutions: If your rear suspension is springing back, go ahead and slow down your rebound damping. Chances are your weight is too high and too far forward. Here's the thing: When you get scared, you unconsciously move your head away from the danger, which elevates your body and makes it hard to get far enough back. Lower your torso (dropping your seat helps) and get your butt back. Amazing! Stop blaming your poor bike.

Problem: Struggling for balance. Maybe you find yourself swinging your bars back and forth and waving your knees all over the place as you try to make a turn or get over an outcropping.

Solutions: Relax. Look as far ahead as possible (don't look at the ground immediately in front of you!). Speed up for greater stability.

Mountain bike riding—the kind where you zoom up steep climbs, bomb descents, and carve through the woods—is actually mountain bike driving. You're not just a passenger; you're also the engine and the pilot. Don't think of your pedals or tires as objects to manipulate; think of them as parts of you. The more comfortable you become with your "extended body," the more you'll get out of your riding . . . er . . . driving.

3

Make Great Power

Bikes are cool because you propel them with your own power. You fly through nature, running on pasta and listening to your breathing. Bikes suck because you propel them with your own power. You labor up hills, trying not to puke and gasping for dear life.

When it comes to making power, most people and publications emphasize fitness. Basically, riding faster and longer enables you to ride even faster and even longer. But no matter how hard we work, we eventually crash into our genetic and motivational ceilings. So, assuming you're already as strong as you can be (or deserve to be), it makes sense to become more efficient. You'll use less energy for the same power, the same energy for more power, or, as your fitness improves, more energy for even more power.

Brian Knows Pedaling

Don't think for a second that because Brian specializes in bikercross, which requires explosive starts and downhill sprints, he can't blast flats and hammer climbs with the best of them.

In fact, B.L. is one of the strongest pedalers in mountain biking—and one of the strongest pedalers in the world. He represented the United States on the 2002 track cycling team. He won the prologue street sprints at the 2000 Redlands Classic road stage race. And he won the downtown time trial at the 2001 Durango World Cup—against all the top cross-country racers.

I can personally vouch for B.L.'s strength. At the 2004 Big Bear national, he was recovering from a broken tibia. He couldn't race the big boys, but he did challenge me to a sprint in front of my condo.

"I have the wrong shoes," I said.

"I have a broken leg."

"Okay, let's do it."

We lined up 50 yards down the street, and my buddy yelled, "Go!"

Crank crank crank crank. In four strokes, Brian was so far ahead he broke into a manual and looked backward to see what I was doing. I maintained full power and still lost by a bike length. I'm a strong pedaler, but B.L. is just ridiculous.

—LMc

Build a Perfect Pedal Stroke

A basic pedal stroke can be simple. You push down and your bike goes forward, right? But excellent pedaling is another story. You need to apply power around a 350-mm circle, with the force perpendicular to the crank arms the whole time. This involves three pairs of major muscles in our legs and hips, as well as dozens of supporting muscles all over our bodies, all firing in perfect sequence, up to twice a second, for hours at a time, against varying resistance, on rough terrain, in dirty shorts . . .

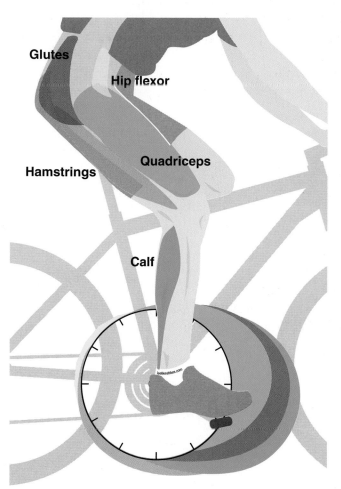

Which muscles are doing the work

In the graph, the thickness of each area shows the relative amount of useful power each muscle produces.

Your quads do most of the work at the top of the stroke. Your glutes and calves take over as your pedal approaches 6 o'clock, then your hamstrings sweep the pedal back to nine o'clock. Your hip flexors help lift the pedal to the top for another go-around.

Adapted from Ericson, et al. 1986. "Power output and work in different muscle groups during ergometer cycling." *European Journal of Applied Physiology and Occupational Physiology*, 229-235.

As you can see, a lot goes on between your little toes. Because a perfect stroke is so complex, it makes sense to break it down and attack one segment at a time. Picture the pedaling rotation as the face of a clock. Pedal strokes vary among riders, depending on their body types, riding position, cadence, and even which type of riding they're doing. The following photos show Gunn-Rita Dahle on a trainer in Boulder, Colorado, during a break from competition. In 2004, she won the World Cup, World, and Olympic cross-country titles, so I guess you can say her stroke will give you some good guidelines. Note: You need clip-in pedals to pedal this way.

Gunn-Rita Dahle, Merida Multivan Racing Team

Down: 1 to 5 O'clock

The vast majority of your pedaling power comes from driving the pedals downward. But this is not a simple downward push. The downstroke involves three directions: forward, down, and backward, each using a different set of muscles.

- Early in the afternoon (before 3 o'clock), use your quads to push your feet forward.

- Later in the afternoon, use your glutes to push your leg downward. There's a lot of power here.

- As you get near the bottom, use your calves to extend your foot and start sweeping the pedal back toward evening. Typically, the higher your seat, the more you extend your foot (Gunn-Rita runs a pretty high seat). With a very low seat (as in downhill racing), your heel might stay beneath your toes.

Back: 5 to 7 O'clock

If you find yourself pushing down at the bottom of your stroke, you are wasting energy and wearing out your pedals (just kidding on the pedals).

- With your toes pointed down a bit, scoop backward with your hamstrings.

- Pretend you're scraping dog crap off the bottom of your shoe. Traditional wisdom says to pretend there's mud on your shoe, but dog crap is more motivating.

Up: 7 to 10 O'clock

The muscles that pull our feet up are so slow and weak that they can't lift one foot fast enough to get out of your downward foot's way. When you spin fast, your pushing leg actually lifts your pulling leg. The best you can do is lighten the load.

- Keep pulling with your hamstrings as you pass the bottom of the stroke. As you pass 9 o'clock, start pulling straight up with your hip flexors. Doing this correctly requires concentration, but you can really feel the added power and smoothness.

- As you stroke upward, lift your toes.

Forward: 10 to 1 O'clock

If you pay attention to your form, you can begin your power stroke way up here, which means you carry more momentum into your downstroke and create more power and better times for all.

- As you sweep upward past 10 o'clock, drive your knees up and forward with your hip flexors.

- Your heel should drop a bit as you reach the top of the clock. With a low seat your heel will be way below your toes. With a high seat your heel might remain above your toes.

- As you pass high noon, begin pushing forward with your quads. Be ready for your rear tire to break loose from all that power!

Pedaling Exercises

Here are some exercises to improve your stroke and break up the monotony of your life. Do each one for 20 seconds to a minute, with easy spinning between. Remember, these are skill drills, not intervals. Focus on technique and save the puking for later. Do these on a trainer or safe road, and be sure to warm up. Oh, and eat your veggies.

One-footed pedaling. Pull one foot out and pedal with the other, trying to maintain tension all the way around the stroke. (1) You'll be amazed at the dead spots and herky-jerkyness. Dang, you really are a horrible pedaler! (2) You'll be amazed when muscles you've never used start jumping in to smooth things out.

High resistance. Put it in a huge gear and pedal slowly, at around 50 to 60 rpm. The resistance will force you to recruit all your muscles to keep things turning, and the slowness will teach your brain to fire off the right messages in the right order. This is also a fantastic power workout.

High rpm. Put it in an easy gear and spin as fast as you can without bouncing off your bike—100, 120, 150 rpm, whatever you can do. This puts a polish on your perfect stroke.

You can hit all three exercises in one session. In the off season, emphasize one-footed pedaling. As you build strength entering the season, emphasize high resistance. As you reach the racing season, emphasize high rpm.

Make Mad Power With These Tips

Master the most powerful segments first.   Your downstroke usually takes care of itself. Pay attention to pushing hard, but not past the bottom of the circle. Next, concentrate on sweeping your pedals across the top. This is the second strongest part of your stroke, and it greatly lengthens the amount of time you actually apply power. Once you get the top dialed, think about bringing your pedals up. Lastly, think about scraping the dog poop off the bottom of your shoes. If all you do is push across the top and down to the bottom, your stroke will be powerful and free of dead spots.

Go for a smooth handoff.　Your muscles shouldn't hand off a baton and then wait around for their next turn. Strive for smooth transitions from segment to segment, muscle to muscle. This is supposed to be a circle, not a rhombus.

Spin.　High cadences (more than 80 rpm) are easy on your legs and give you plenty of snap.

Loud legs, quiet body.　Use only the muscles that carry you up the hill. Any other tension is wasted. After you stop hunching your shoulders and death-gripping your bar, try relaxing your quads on the upstroke.

Stabilize your core.　Your abdominal muscles create a stable connection between your torso and hips. If you leave your core loose, you lose power in the sway between your hips and shoulders, and you might give yourself a bonus backache. When you use your lower abs to help pull your legs up, their tension will help stabilize your core. With your lower abs tight like this, your upper belly can still balloon out for breathing.

Breathe with your belly.　Try to breathe slowly and deeply, and let your belly expand as you draw air with your diaphragm. You should look like you have a little pooch—if you don't have one already!

Pedaling is pedaling.　These ideas apply whether you're laboring up the 401 trail in Crested Butte, hammering a roller at the Olympic cross-country course, blasting out of a starting gate, or going for the recumbent land-speed record.

Do it right, before it's too late.　If you've been pedaling bikes for 10 years for five hours a week at 80 rpm, you've turned more than 10 million strokes. If you've done them all poorly, you have some very bad habits to overcome. From the standpoint of creating a great stroke, short and sweet is better than long and sloppy. If you get so tired your stroke turns to a rhombus, call it quits for the day or go Rollerblading to finish your workout.

In the Saddle

Seated pedaling carries you up long hills and across expansive flats in the most efficient way. Pedal from your plastic perch whenever possible, and keep these notions in mind:

Use your seat.　As you push your pedals forward across the top of your stroke, push your butt back against your saddle. When you push the pedals really hard, pull lightly on the bars to help hold you steady and transmit that power to the ground.

Maintain traction.   Move back on your saddle when your rear wheel slips and forward when your front wheel wanders. If you're climbing a steep, slippery pitch, keep your butt back for rear traction and pull your shoulders forward to keep weight on the front tire. When you begin a steep pitch, it's safest to start with your weight way back on the bike to keep the rear wheel tracking. If your front end wanders, just steer it back on track and nudge your weight forward.

Give 'em a rest.   Shift forward or back to use different muscles. Move forward to emphasize your quads. Move back to work your hamstrings and glutes. By shifting the work around, you can stay strong as long as King Kong.

Out of the Saddle

Your back is getting sore. You want to carry speed over a short rise. Your buddy just took off for the trail sign. Sometimes you gotta stand up and make some extra power. When your butt leaves the saddle, your perfect pedal stroke tends to leave as well. Don't let it.

Dance on the pedals.   You've no doubt heard television announcer Phil Ligget wax poetic about Lance Armstrong's standing climbfests in the 2003 Tour de France. When Lance stood, his stroke stayed as perfect as when he sat. He pulled his pedals up, swept them across the top, and pushed them down in one constant flow. If you pause at the bottom of your stroke, Lance will come to your house and kick your ass. Don't pause. Keep 'em turning.

Pull it.   Counteract your massive power strokes by pulling the bars and rocking your bike from side to side. Women can dramatically improve their power by learning to use their upper bodies this way.

Even more abs.   Use your core muscles to stabilize your torso and transmit torque from your shoulders to your hips. Don't fall into the trap of building strong arms and legs and ignoring the bridge that connects them.

Upshift.   Your standing power will crush your sitting gear like a bug. If you click it up a notch, you'll maintain traction, preserve form, and go faster—which is always good. Bonus speed trick: On a climb with steep corners and great traction, try standing and upshifting around the turns.

Stand up straight.   When there's enough traction, try to stand erect, with your hips forward and your shoulders directly above your hips. This way, you don't waste lower-back effort to pull your torso up, plus you put max power into your pedals.

When your tires are gripping, stand above your pedals and drive straight down from your hip.

Dynamic traction

Pulling back on the bars during your downstroke lifts the front end and levers the rear wheel into the ground.

Front tire is light and fork is extended.

Weight slightly forward of bottom bracket.

This pitch on A River Runs Through It in Whistler, British Columbia, requires hard pedaling and a soft touch.

No, crouch.   When traction isn't so hot or the terrain is rough, crouch on your bike. Move up and down as you cross obstacles and scoot forward or backward to maintain traction.

Get some dynamic traction.   The trails in Laguna Beach, California, have some really steep, slippery, technical sections that only a few people can ride. You have to be in the right gear—not so hard you can't spin it and not so easy your back tire burns out. To clean a steep, slippery climb, crouch down and forward with your head and shoulders above your bars. With each power stroke, pull strongly and smoothly on the bars. This unweights your front wheel and levers your rear wheel into the ground for extra grip. Bonus: Pulling hard lets you pull a taller gear than usual, which gives you an extra-long, extra-smooth power stroke. And everybody likes that.

Sprinting

On long climbs you gotta spin as efficiently as possible. No sense working any harder than you need to, eh? But sprinting is all about max power. Whether you're charging off the line, blasting over a rise, or passing a foe, there's more to sprinting than just pedaling as hard as you can.

The right gear is more important than ever. Sprints happen soon and hard. When you only have time for a few strokes, you better make them count.

Attack it all at once. Commit 100 percent to turning those pedals and getting up to speed as quickly as possible. Try to reach your max rpm in as few strokes as possible. Try for 10, then 5.

Push down like a maniac. Perfect circles can wait 'til after you get up to speed. For now, concentrate on the downstroke.

Use your whole body. Yank on the bars as you push the pedals. This is mostly a biceps and lat trick, but try using your pecs to pull the grips across your chest. Keep your torso rigid for max power transfer.

Don't shift too soon. Wait until you're about to wind the gear out, then shift. Repeat.

Set up your bike like a BMXer. Compared with a stretched-out cross-country setup, a shorter stem, higher bars, and low seat let you get lower behind the pedals, where you can pull up on the bars more powerfully and begin your power stroke earlier. It's harder to get up to speed on an XC bike with the seat all up in your business.

© Shawn Spomer

Brian lays down the power in 4X racing action. Check out that grimace!

Spin to Win

One of the age-old questions is, should I spin easy gears or grind hard ones? Well, that depends.

Everybody has different leg strength, knee health, and pedaling skill. Some of us spin easy gears, and some of us pull harder gears. (The strongest of us spin hard gears.) Look at Jan Ullrich and Lance Armstrong: Ullrich churns the butter while Armstrong whips the cream, yet both guys are insanely fast in the climbs and time trials.

Winding It Up With Brian

When I was in Japan (in October 2003), they had this sprinting machine. It was a stationary bike tied to a computer to see how fast you could get it going. The gear wasn't hard. It only took about four seconds to wind it up and you were done. That was as fast as you could spin. Some kirin racer had the record with 76.7 kph. It took me six or seven tries to hit 77.4 kph.

Brian Takes on Big Papa

My buddy and I were riding moto in SoCal one day, and all of a sudden we decided to go to Phoenix for the Supercross. I hauled home, got on a plane, and we were there. After the race, we were hanging out in front of the stadium. There were all these guys with pedicabs—you know, the bikes with trailers attached to them, like rickshaws.

I challenged one of the guys to a race. He was like, sure, for how much? I said I dunno, how about something interesting, like $100? He said okay and unhooked his bike. I borrowed some beater to ride. This bike was so clapped out, I was afraid to pedal hard, like it would break in half or something.

Dude, I gated the guy bad. In like 30 feet I was already 20 feet ahead. I just started zig-zagging and looking back at him. It was so funny. When he handed over the money, he was like, "Dang, you're pretty fast. Do you race?" I said, well, a little bit when I was a kid.

He called over the guy who owns the company, "Big Papa"—it said that on the seat of his pedicab. He challenged me to a race: double or nothing. I said sure, I'll go for that. I got another bike; this one was even worse, a totally jacked-up Huffy. I dusted him just as bad, and I paid for my whole trip with just a couple little sprints!

Brian poses with his loot—and the winning machine.

Each of us has our own personal powerband, the rpm range where we pedal smoothly and powerfully. When the gear's too easy, your legs bounce up and down like you're chopping wood. When the gear's too hard, you bog down like a woolly mammoth in tar.

The broader you make your powerband, the better. You want to be neither a stump-pulling diesel tractor nor a high-revving two-stroke motocrosser. You want to be a finely tuned Chevy small block: plenty of pop off the line, smooth midrange for extended power, and gobs of high-end speed.

For steady power, a high cadence places the burden on your aerobic system and lets your legs spin easy. At the same speed, fit riders last far longer at 90 rpm than they do at 60 rpm. Experiment to find your optimum cadence. In deep sand, stay on top of a small gear. On wet moss, filter your power through a tall gear. You might spin fast and light in the beginning of a ride, then slog slow and heavy as you get tired.

As your stroke gets smoother, your cadence will increase. When you first start riding, it takes all your concentration to churn along at 60 rpm. After a few years of concentrated practice, you can buzz along at 100 rpm and sprint past 120 rpm.

When it's time to accelerate, wind those legs as fast as they'll go. If you can make power from 60 to 120 rpm, you can double your speed in the same gear. Shifting means changing your grip, backing off the pressure, and risking a case of chain-fu. So less shifting is better shifting—as long as you're making good power. How many racing engines make their power at low rpm? None. They spin to win—just like you do. Here's your homework:

1. Learn to spin as fast as possible.

2. Experiment to find your optimum cadence.

3. Use a gear that keeps you at your optimum cadence.

Shift Like a Champ

Mountain bike drive trains can be confusing. With 27 gears and four levers, where do you start?

Shifting 101.   Use your rear shifter to fine-tune your gear ratio and keep yourself spinning in your powerband. Save front shifts for major terrain changes.

○ Big ring: Downhill and fast, flat riding

○ Middle ring: Short or mellow climbs and slow, flat riding

○ Small ring: Long or steep climbs

Keep your chain straight.   You can theoretically run your chain all the way from your small ring to your small cog or your big ring to your big cog, but doing so invites chain skippage, extra friction, and faster wear. You can hit all of your ratios without crossing your chain.

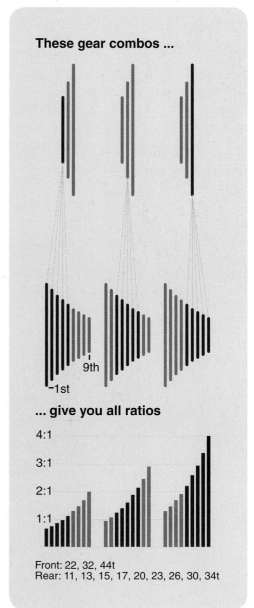

These gear combos ...

9th

1st

... give you all ratios

4:1

3:1

2:1

1:1

Front: 22, 32, 44t
Rear: 11, 13, 15, 17, 20, 23, 26, 30, 34t

- If you're in your big ring and you want to downshift from your fifth cog to your fourth-largest cog, drop it to your middle ring and sixth cog.

- If you're in your middle ring and you want to upshift from your seventh to eighth cog, grab the big ring and fourth cog.

- If you're in your middle ring and third cog, and you want a slightly easier gear, drop to your small ring and fifth cog.

- If you're in your small ring and you want a gear taller than your fifth cog, grab your middle ring and third cog.

If this is all too much for you to comprehend, leave it in your middle ring. Your rear gear range will get you through most situations. As a matter of fact, many strong downhillers run single rings with chain guides on their cross-country bikes so they can charge like demons and not worry about losing their chains. Coast the fast descents and, if you must, walk the steep climbs.

Keep it tight.   For a given gear ratio, use the biggest ring and cog you can without crossing your chain. This tightens your chain and spreads the load over more teeth. A violent sprint can tear a chain right off a small ring.

Shift before you need to.   High-end rear derailleurs can handle a lot of pressure, but even the best front shifters can crumble under your awesome power. Surge for half a crank, back off a bit, make your shift, and then get back on it.

Shoot Your Troubles

Problem: Your legs burn, especially at the beginning of your ride.

Solution: Warm up. Take it easy for 10 minutes or so then gradually up the intensity. Lions don't warm up before they run down antelopes, but they don't run for hours, now do they?

Problem: Your quads are getting really tired.

Solution: Move back on the saddle and concentrate on pushing forward and pulling back. This emphasizes your glutes and hamstrings and provides a bit of rest to your four best friends.

Problem: You're struggling and feel really uncomfortable on a climb.

Solution: Pay attention to your form. Open your upper body, lighten your hands, and spin smooth circles. This can make a huge difference. That said, if you're going super hard or you're out of shape, it's gonna hurt. Welcome to cycling.

Problem: When you climb out of the saddle, your triceps get tired from leaning on the bars.

Solution: Move your hips back so your weight moves exclusively to your feet. For extended climbing, rest your hands neutrally on the bars. For max power, pull on the bars with each downstroke.

Problem: Your chain falls off on downhills.

Solution: Descend in your big chainring and one of the middle to larger cogs. Remove links until your chain is barely long enough for your big ring/big cog combo. If the tighter chain doesn't do the trick, think about installing a chain guide.

Problem: You feel tired and weak.

Solution: You *are* tired and weak. Get off your butt and train! But don't overdo it, or you'll dig yourself a deeper hole.

You've heard the old adage "work smarter, not harder." We encourage you to train so you can pedal harder, but you'll enjoy free speed by learning to pedal smarter. Just as you shouldn't hurl yourself off cliffs hoping you'll learn to land, you shouldn't mash your cranks hoping you'll become a great pedaler. Pay attention to your pedal stroke. A great spin is a bike rider's greatest asset.

4

Brake Better to Go Faster

You roll across a mountain meadow. Butterflies flit among the daffodils, and your rotors spin freely through your calipers. Suddenly you see a rare caterpillar and hit your brakes. Well, mister, you've just started a battle—a battle of friction.

If your pads grip your rotors better than your tires grip the ground, the brakes win: Your wheels lock, and you skid right past the Rocky Mountain leaf sucker. But if your tires find traction, they force a compromise: They let the wheels keep turning, but more and more slowly until you release the brakes, and you stop and cram that wiggly sucker into a plastic bag.

Good braking makes you fast. When you carry the right speed into corners and technical sections, you carry a higher speed out. Here are some good reasons to slow down:

- Maintain a legal, socially responsible speed. We can't overstress the importance of obeying those 15 mph speed limits. But seriously, don't be an idiot. Share the trail, share the world, man.

- Maintain control, especially in rough conditions. If you're going so fast you can't see straight, it's okay to slow down (a bit). Slow and in control equals good. Fast and random equal bad.

- Set up for a corner. The faster you enter the corner, the harder it is to make the corner. Twice as fast is four times as hard. So slow down—unless you enjoy skidding into poison oak.

Become a master of brake science with these tips:

Reduce your perceived speed.   Most of us brake when we feel like we're going too fast, even when we aren't going fast at all. To take the edge off that "oh my . . ." feeling, look farther ahead. It's that simple. The threats won't seem as immediate.

The less time you spend braking, the better.   When you get on the binders, bad things happen. Tires skip. Suspensions stiffen. Wheels bash. Muscles tighten. When you brake, brake hard, then get back to coasting. Brakes are like pints of Ben & Jerry's ice cream: Fun at the right times but bad news when you use them all the time.

Give it the finger, but which ones?   If you have strong, well-set-up brakes, your index fingers should do the trick. If you need to brake extra hard, give it your middle finger too.

Brake in a straight line.   Your tires must be perpendicular to the ground. If you brake with your tires leaned, they'll either stand up or slide out. Neither is cool.

Brake on good ground.   Look for smooth spots with good traction. I (Brian) have been down hills that were so steep and where the traction was so good, that as I slowed down gobs of dirt fell on me. Trying to slow down in slippery muck just sketches you out and wastes valuable finger fu.

Use both brakes.   The front tire gets the most traction, so you can and should squeeze the front brake harder than the rear. Finesse the rear to keep it from skidding. By the way, don't be afraid of the front brake. You have to do some stupid stuff—simultaneously brake hard, lean forward, and hit something   to fly over the bars.

Ease into it.   Sudden, hard braking leads to skidding, which leads to marijuana and then to heavier drugs, not to mention longer stopping distances. A rolling tire offers far more traction than a skidding tire. Squeeze the levers slowly to gradually build up the braking force. If a tire starts to break loose, ease the pressure on that brake or put more weight on that tire. The most powerful braking happens at the point just before a skid.

Practice braking as hard as you can without skidding.   Experiment with body position and lever pressure. Know how long it takes to slow down on a variety of surfaces. The more confidently you can haul yourself down quickly and safely, the faster you'll ride and the less time you'll waste lightly dragging the brakes.

Get back and down.   Any time you brake, get off your saddle and lean back to counter your forward momentum. When you brake hard, get down low to focus your weight on the pedals and increase rear traction. When you brake really hard on steep descents, drop your heels so your feet are behind your pedals.

Never lock your front wheel.   You need your front wheel to steer, and when it's skidding it's not steering. If the front wheel starts to lock, ease off the brake until it starts to roll again.

Modulate or die.   Rocks, roots, holes, sand, gravel, and mud give your front wheel lots of opportunities to get stuck or lock up. When it gets rough or loose, you must constantly modulate the brake. On where it's smooth or sticky, off where it's rough or slippery. If you're about to roll off a big rock, brake hard before the rock and then let your wheel roll freely over it.

Load your tires.   By doubling the weight on your tires, you can double your traction and cut your stopping distance in half. Bounce up a bit to unweight your tires, then push your bike down and forward as you apply the brakes. Really cram your tires into the ground. You'll be amazed at how hard you can brake without skidding.

Know Your Stopping Distance

To brake in the right places and times, you need to know how much space you need to slow down or stop. Your braking sense will develop with experience, but it never hurts to seed your brain with some unpopped kernels:

It's all math, baby!   Stopping distance is a product of your tires, suspension, brake power, ground surface, weight distribution, and your speed. And let's not forget skill.

Bike setup.   When it comes to gripping the ground, high-pressure semislick tires are rebellious teenagers, and low-pressure knobbies are first-day preschoolers;

Brian Likes Brakes

Brakes are really important. The feel and position and how well they work is what I'm most picky about—even more than bar height and other setup things. Strong brakes aren't super important for cross-country because you're winning on the climbs, not by pushing your brakes to the limit in corners, so lighter is probably best. Strong brakes are most important on downhill bikes because you can go faster by carrying speed farther into a turn and braking later.

Nose Wheelies

Hit your front brake as you lunge forward. See how long you can stay up there. This teaches general bike control, and it comes in handy when you want to nose-wheelie around a switchback (see "Conquer Switchbacks" in chapter 5).

they grab onto dirt like it's their mommy. Long-travel bikes with active suspension designs hook up best, and disc brakes just plain rule. Any setup change will affect your braking, so dial your bike the way you like it and ride, ride, ride!

Rolling friction.   In soft, deep dirt, your bike plows like a lazy horse, so you don't need to brake all that much. As in powder skiing, you can point it downhill and let all the little particles modulate your speed. On hardpack, your bike rolls faster than an AMF Triumph TNT bowling ball, so all slowing must come from your brakes (or bashing into pins—not cool).

Braking traction.   At 10 miles per hour on dry concrete, it takes about four feet to stop. Wet concrete ups the distance to six feet (a 50 percent increase). Sand drops the distance to five feet. Sand provides way less braking traction than wet or dry concrete, but its high rolling friction does a lot of scrubbing. Ice is the worst: low traction plus fast rolling equals a stopping distance of 29 feet.* You can optimize traction by shifting your weight backward the right amount, and you can double or triple your traction by loading your tires as you brake.

Speed kills.   When you plug speed into the equation for braking distance (or cornering or crashing) it has a huge effect on the outcome. If you cut your traction in half, you double your braking distance. No big deal. If you double your speed, you *quadruple* your stopping distance. So the faster you go, the more important it is that you plan ahead—and the more important you load your tires for maximum traction.

Control Your Excess Braking

Do you pedal just for the heck of it, when you don't really need to speed up? Of course not. So why do you brake for no reason?

Blame fear. Most of us scrub speed whenever we feel nervous. Those levers are like our little blankie; they comfort us and tell us we're in control. The thing is, while we're on the brakes we usually have less control. Dragging them makes your bike unruly. Grabbing them makes you crash.

Try to brake only when there's a real reason to slow down. If you're nervous with your speed, don't drag the brakes. Instead, brake hard to slow way down, then let your bike roll. When you feel sketchy again, shut it back down.

Riding problems seldom arise from not braking often enough. They usually come from braking too often. In sketchy situations, you're just a twitch away from an over-the-bars calamity. Sometimes the only solution is to take those itchy trigger fingers and wrap them around your grips.

We're not suggesting you always fist your bars, but it does make sense in certain situations. On mellow descents or in fast race sections, fist both bars. In gnarly situations, like steep drops over wet roots, cover your rear brake but wrap your front-brake finger around the grip. Your rear brake will help you control your speed, but your front brake would spell disaster. If you really need your brakes,

*Calculations inspired by the Science of Cycling Web site, © Exploratorium, www. exploratorium.edu

you'll have plenty of time to grab them: If an obstacle pops up on the trail, you should be looking far enough ahead to react to it; if you hit a patch of ice or something, braking is the last thing you want to do. If you drag the brakes because you feel like you should be doing *something*, try pumping the bumps or even pedaling instead.

Remember: Braking is the number-one way to mess up your bike's handling: (1) Braking forces you to move to the back of your cockpit, which messes with your balance. If you let off the brakes and try to turn with your weight still too far back, your front wheel will wander like a stringless kite. (2) Braking eats up part of your "traction pie," which leaves less adhesion for cornering. (3) With your wheels unable to spin freely, your bike bashes into bumps instead of rolling and skimming over them. (4) Some suspension designs lock out under hard braking. When this happens, you bash into bumps even harder, which is not good.

Stick this to your refrigerator: Brake hard to slow down, then get back to coasting.

Battle Braking Bumps

Right now, thousands of riders are braking for corners. Their skipping tires are scooping up dirt and piling it into humps. What begins as brown corduroy grows into huge whoops that randomize bikes and beat brains out. Braking bumps form where most people want to brake, and the harder you brake on them, the worse off you are. So what to do?

Here it is: Do not brake on braking bumps. Just because everyone else braked in the same place doesn't mean you have to. There are lots of better places to brake:

1. **Outside the bumps.** Consider this the hot tip. You brake on fresh ground, plus you get a wider entrance to the turn. Both good things.

2. **Inside the bumps.** When there's no room on the outside, you can brake on the inside of the bumps and then dive into the corner. This makes for a tight turn, but it can be better to fly past huge bumps, brake hard, and then deal with your "acute" turning situation. (Ha! A geometry joke!)

3. **Before the bumps.** If you insist on following the bumpy line but would rather skim over the little bastards than bash into them, brake before the bumps and coast loosely over them. This will cost you speed, but you'll gain comfort. This works fine for leisure riding.

This is a really bad place to grab your front brake. That's why Marla Streb is fisting her left grip.

These braking bumps are gnarly. The funny thing is, you don't have to brake for this sweet berm.

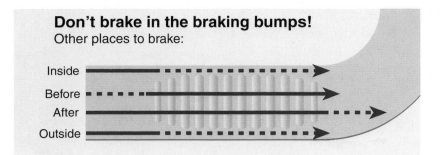

Don't brake in the braking bumps!
Other places to brake:

Inside

Before

After

Outside

4. After the bumps. That's right: after. Most riders brake too soon and too long, and you end up with big bumps way before the corner and little to no bumps near the corner. Skim over the main bumps, pinch those eight-inch discs, and then fold into the corner.

When the only decent braking spots have bumps, you have no choice but to grab the levers, stay loose, and use your suspension. Pay attention to the bumps and try to brake hardest where it's smoothest.

Brian Schools Lee in the Way of Braking Bumps

I'd been chasing Brian down Whistler's trails for a couple of days, and I was feeling pretty studly. On our hundredth run down the A-Line trail, I asked him to follow me and offer me any advice he might have.

I took off, following the main line over a jump, through some rough braking bumps, into a berm, and into the next jump. It felt good, but Brian was yelling, "Stop, stop! That was terrible!"

I hauled down my SX, and he pulled up. "Why did you ride over all those bumps?"

"I dunno," I answered. "That's where the line is."

We walked back to the section, and he showed me how I could go around the bumps to the inside. Since there was a nice berm, I could still make the corner just fine. On the next run, I did just that, and it felt way smoother and faster.

Shoot Your Troubles

Problem: Your rear tire skids too easily.

Solution: Shift your weight backward. Use less rear brake. Try a bigger, knobbier rear tire.

Problem: Your front tire skids. (With your front tire, any skidding is bad skidding.)

Solution: Shift your weight forward. Use less front brake, especially in loose conditions. Try a bigger, knobbier front tire. Only brake in a straight line.

Problem: On rough terrain your front wheel gets stuck and pitches you forward.

Solution: Use the brakes on smooth ground and absolutely, positively, stay off them while your front wheel rolls over rough ground.

Problem: When you do lots of serious downhilling, your knuckles ache. The backs of your forearms might burn as well.

Solution: Adjust your brake levers closer to your grips so you don't have to reach as far.

Your brakes are the most powerful control mechanism on your bike. Just think of it: You can haul down more than 200 pounds of speeding meat and metal with just a little pressure from your index fingers. Now that's power. But your binders are far more than on-off switches for your rolling wheels. A light touch gives you complete control over your speed: You can slow down for a rock, stop in front of an alligator, or set up for a series of corners.

5

Carve Any Corner

© Josh McGuckin

The sun is shining and so is your new XTR crank set. It's a beautiful day after a rain, and the soil is as tacky as a fresh motocross track. You and your friends rail along your favorite singletrack. You fly down a straight, float atop the braking bumps, hit the brakes, and then fold into a flat, sweeping left. You carve so hard, sweat flies sideways in front of your glasses. Sweet.

Corners separate fun trails from boring ones and great riders from so-so ones. To corner well is to enjoy the best trails in the world.

Master the Basics of Every Turn

You could fill an entire set of encyclopedias with all possible combinations of turn radius, camber, and elevation, but you can break every turn into four steps: the setup, the entrance, the turn itself, and the exit.

Set Up the Turn

Successful cornering depends on good lines, and lines begin before you reach the turn.

Look as far as you can into the turn.   If you're noodling along on a twisty singletrack, you'll peek 10 feet around a redwood trunk. If you're hauling the mail down Vermont's Mt. Snow downhill course, you'll scan along the tape 100 feet ahead. Check out the surface and the worn lines. Decide where you want to enter the turn and where to start braking.

Get on your line.   Your corner has already begun. Line up on the inside, middle, or outside, depending on the line you plan to follow (see "Follow the Right Lines," page 57).

Judge your speed.   It takes practice to learn how hot you can bake different corners. The worse the traction and the tighter the radius, the slower you have to go. The better the traction and the wider the turn radius, the faster you can go. But beware: As your speed increases, the turning g-forces increase exponentially. That means twice the speed makes a turn four times as hard to make. Err on the slow side unless the ground is tacky or the turn is banked.

Slow down while you're still going straight.   Brake late and hard so you spend more time at speed. Enter the turn slowly so you can accelerate past the apex and exit with max speed.

Enter the Turn

Now it's time to initiate your corner. You'll lean into sweeping turns delicately, like you're opening your grandmother's photo album. You'll fold into tight turns as if you're slamming a phone book shut . . . bam!

Let off the brakes.   At the very least, let off your front brake. Most riders dive into corners, get nervous, and grab a shipload of Shimano. Their

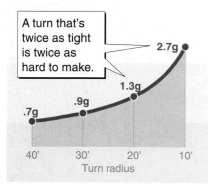

Tight turns are harder to make
Side forces in a 20-mph

A turn that's twice as tight is twice as hard to make.

2.7g
1.3g
.9g
.7g

40'   30'   20'   10'
Turn radius

As you go faster, turning becomes much harder
Side forces in a turn with a 20-foot radius. Gnarly roller coasters achieve 3.0 g's.

3.0g

1.3g

Doubling your speed quadruples the side force.

.3g

10 mph   20 mph   30 mph

How Bikes Turn

At low speeds, you steer your bike by turning your handlebars in the direction you want to go. At high speeds, you lean your bike in the direction you want to go. Leaning is much more reliable than steering. When you steer your wheel, your tire basically bashes into irregularities in the ground and deflects in the direction you want to turn. When you lean a tire, it rolls around the turn like a rubber-edged ice cream cone. Steered tires want to slide. Leaned tires want to rail.

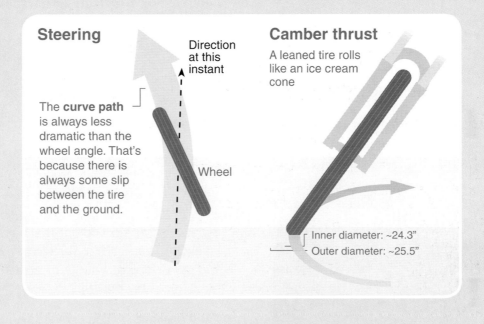

Steering

Direction at this instant

The **curve path** is always less dramatic than the wheel angle. That's because there is always some slip between the tire and the ground.

Wheel

Camber thrust

A leaned tire rolls like an ice cream cone

Inner diameter: ~24.3"
Outer diameter: ~25.5"

bikes stand up and follow a tangent into the poison oak, or they slide out. If you wake up tomorrow and decide to lay off your brakes in corners, your riding will improve instantly and dramatically.

Lean into the turn.   The faster and the tighter the turn, the more you have to lean. See "Lean to the Right Degree" on page 59.

Look where you're going.   In the California Motorcycle Safety Foundation's classes, they teach the "big head turn." As you begin the turn, scan along the trail toward the exit. Go ahead and notice important details, but keep your eyes moving through the turn. Scary obstacles want you to stare at them. You must resist. When you turn your head, your body unconsciously leans that way, and the bike follows right along.

Be patient.   If you're out riding a new trail, don't dive straight into the insides of corners. It's safer and usually faster to enter wide and have a look before you initiate your turn. (Check out the lines section on page 57.)

Slow, Look, Lean, Roll

That's what the Motorcycle Safety Foundation teaches its road-riding students.

1. Slow down as you approach the turn.

2. Look through the turn for the best line.

3. Lean into the turn.

4. Roll the throttle.

   Since we don't have that throttle thing, let's slow, look, lean, carve.

As long as you let your front tire do its job, your rear tire can afford a little vacation.

Make the Turn

While you're carving your corner, your job is to maintain traction and hold your line. Remember that cornering is dynamic: You'll cross different surfaces, and you hit things. If you try to rigidly maintain any one position on your bike, you will get deflected, and you'll follow a tangent into a cactus. Instead, keep your arms and legs loose and project your head and torso in the direction you want to go. Let your body move so your bike can stay in its groove.

Lower your center of gravity.   How many Formula One cars have you seen with lift kits? None, that's how many. Squat as low as you can. Lower your head to your bars. If your seat is low, drop your hips as low as you can. If your seat is high, slide your butt back and drop your shoulders so your torso spreads above the seat.

Distribute your weight.   Stay balanced between the front and rear of your bike, but:

- If you feel the front end pushing (sliding out), lean forward to increase front-wheel traction.

- If you feel the rear end starting to slide out, lean backward to help it catch. That said, if your rear tire really lets go, lean forward to make your front tire dig in. As long as your front wheel keeps tracking, you'll probably make the turn.

Lay off the brakes!   If you're overbaking it, you can use some rear brake to slow down and maybe skid the rear end around. But don't touch the front brake, no matter what. If you do grab a fingerful, your front wheel will wash out and you'll crash, or your bike will stand straight up and you'll blow the corner. Either way is a bummer.

Load it.   You can dramatically increase traction by pressing your bike down while you carve your turns. Press slowly and gradually for long, mellow turns and pump violently for abrupt turns. Many great riders, especially downhill and slalom racers, seem to bounce in and out of tight turns. As they enter a turn, they hop slightly to unweight the tires, and then they cram their tires into the apex, achieving max load and max traction.

In a series of turns, load the turns then use the light moment between them to swing your bike in the other direction. It feels exactly like powder skiing: heavy right, light middle, heavy left, light middle . . . on and on down the trail.

Loading a turn   Learn this move. It's your key to cornering faster in all conditions.

1. Drop your weight as you approach your turning point.   2. As you make the turn, press into the ground for increased traction.

Light between turns   This trick helps you transition between close corners. Technical singletrack will never be the same.

1. Load the first turn.   2. Unload. Steer and lean into the next turn.   3. Drop into the next turn and repeat. Stoked!

Exit the Turn

The end of your corner is just the beginning of the next thing. If a straight follows, wait for your bike to straighten out and then start pedaling. If another corner follows, you should already be setting up for it. A clean exit is the most important part of a corner, and it depends on everything that came before it.

Follow the Right Lines

Good lines make for smoothness, speed, and ease. Bad lines make for jerkiness, slowness, and struggle. When you go through a corner, try to make your line as wide as possible. This reduces the violence under your tires and lets you carry maximum speed to the exit of the turn.

You can choose from three basic approaches, each with its good and bad points.

Dive Inside

With an "early apex" or "early entrance," you enter fast on the inside and dive right into the corner.

Good: You carry max speed into the turn. You can protect the inside line from some badger who's trying to pass you. (See the passing section in chapter 11, page 164.)

If You Must Slow Down in a Turn

If you drop your cell phone while you're railing a corner, apply the front brake gradually while standing the bike up and straightening your line.

Bad: You must make a tight turn after the apex—on ground you haven't seen. You tend to overshoot the corner or stall on exit. This is the line for eager juniors: They rush into the turn all excited and then blow their speed.

Early apexes will ruin most turns except those that open up as you go through them (they're called increasing radius turns). If you have room to drift outside on the exit, an early apex works fine. When a fast section leads through a turn and then into a slow section, like a rock garden, go ahead and carry max speed directly into the inside of the corner. Your slow exit speed won't hurt you because you have to slow down for the rocks anyway.

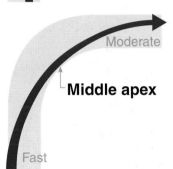

Early apex

Carve a Smooth Arc

With a middle apex, you enter from the outside with moderate speed, carve past the middle of the turn, and exit wide. In a consistent turn with good traction, a middle apex will carry you faster than any other line.

Good: This is the mathematically perfect line. You carry the most speed through the entire turn.

Bad: You can't see the exit very well. Poor traction and unseen obstacles can give you trouble.

Middle apex

Square It Off

With a late apex, you slow down, enter wide, initiate your turn, and then accelerate to the exit.

Good: You can see farther through the turn before you commit to a line. You go relatively straight on the exit. You can start pedaling earlier and carry max speed out of the turn. This is the line for cagey veteran experts: They know when to take it slow, and they save their pop for when it counts. When there's no room to drift outward on the exit, a late apex is the only way to go.

Bad: Nothing.

Late apex

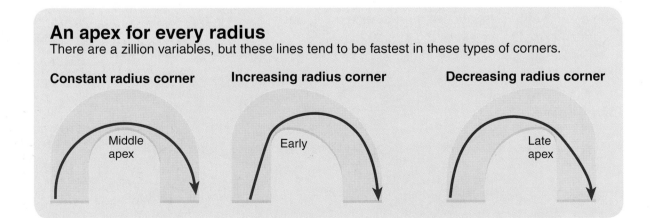

An apex for every radius
There are a zillion variables, but these lines tend to be fastest in these types of corners.

Constant radius corner   **Increasing radius corner**   **Decreasing radius corner**

Middle apex   Early   Late apex

Although a middle apex is often faster, a late apex is safer. Use it on strange trails, in sloppy conditions, and when you don't mind someone sneaking by on the inside. When a straight follows the corner, square it off early and start pedaling as soon as you can.

Don't be afraid to change your mind—or your line. If you see a rock to avoid or a bank to bash into, go for it!

Series of Turns

You zoom along the bottom of Mt. Charleston near Las Vegas. The apron of high desert sweeps for miles in every direction. Joshua trees stand everywhere, like people with their hands in their pockets. The trail winds among them, a big-ring slalom with no end in sight. You're on autopilot: left . . . right . . . left . . . right—but you don't notice the tight chicane ahead. You sweep through the left, then—whoa!—you've already blown the right, and you smash into those swordlike leaves.

Twisty trails can force you to alter your normal lines. You see, the best line for the first turn frequently messes you up for the next one. The last turn in the series is the most important; compromise the others to set yourself up properly.

When in doubt, enter wide and square off the first turn. For example, in a left-then-right series, enter on the far right, cut across the first apex, and then exit as far left as possible to set up for the right turn.

In a series of very tight turns, aim your head and body in a straight line and let the bike turn under you. Think of yourself as a head floating down the trail.

Lean to the Right Degree

To rail turns, you have to fling your body to the inside of your tires, teasing gravity and momentum into a stalemate. The tighter and faster the turn, the more you must lean. If you're falling to the inside, you're leaning too much. If you blow through the turn, you aren't leaning enough.

The last turn is the most important

Late apex in first turn allows smooth middle apex in second (constant radius) turn.

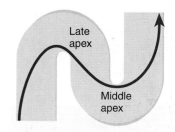

Late apex in first turn allows late apex in second (decreasing radius) turn. Time to pedal!

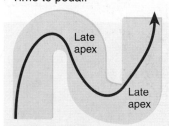

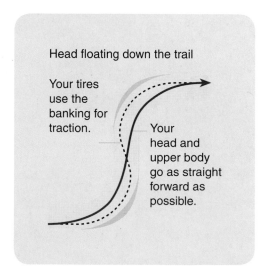

Head floating down the trail

Your tires use the banking for traction.

Your head and upper body go as straight forward as possible.

G-forces and lean angles for various turns

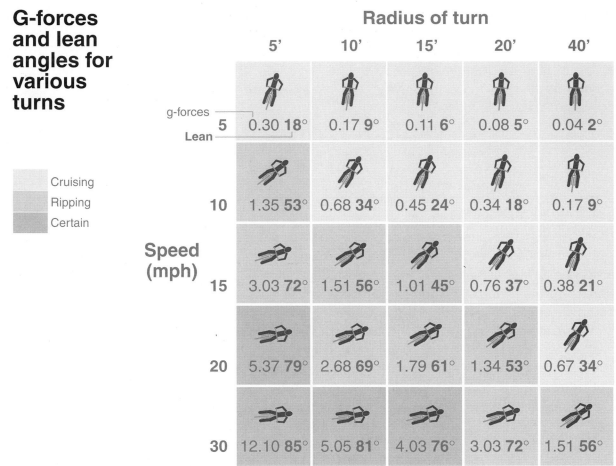

	Radius of turn				
Speed (mph)	**5'**	**10'**	**15'**	**20'**	**40'**
5	0.30 **18°**	0.17 **9°**	0.11 **6°**	0.08 **5°**	0.04 **2°**
10	1.35 **53°**	0.68 **34°**	0.45 **24°**	0.34 **18°**	0.17 **9°**
15	3.03 **72°**	1.51 **56°**	1.01 **45°**	0.76 **37°**	0.38 **21°**
20	5.37 **79°**	2.68 **69°**	1.79 **61°**	1.34 **53°**	0.67 **34°**
30	12.10 **85°**	5.05 **81°**	4.03 **76°**	3.03 **72°**	1.51 **56°**

g-forces
Lean

Cruising
Ripping
Certain

Lean with your bike when you cruise a nice berm.

The above chart shows the g-forces and your lean angle for a variety of turns and speeds. Did you know that when you rail a berm with a 15-foot radius at 15 miles per hour, you're pulling 1 g and leaning 45 degrees? Well, you are. This might seem like nerdiness for nerdiness' sake, but this knowledge can be useful. If you're not sure how fast you can go through a turn, stop and check out the banking. If the angle of the berm (or rut or little ridge) matches your speed and the radius of the turn, then go for it with confidence. Of course, you can go faster than the banking allows, but you'll need gobs of traction.

For every combination of radius and speed, there is only one lean angle that balances turning forces with the force of gravity. You can achieve the same amount of lean in a few different ways, and each way works best in different situations.

Lean your bike and body together.   When your lean angle matches the angle of a berm, you can press directly through the tires and just plain rail the corner. Leaning with your bike works in flat corners, but only when the ground is as sticky as that Clif Shot dribbling from the corner of your mouth.

Lean your bike more than your body. This position gives you extra traction and stability in flat and off-camber corners, or any time your lean exceeds the angle of the ground. Weight your outside pedal. That levers your tires into the ground, so slipping doesn't happen. This is the best cornering position for any turn whose traction might let you down.

Lean your body more than your bike. Less bike lean presses more meat into the ground, which you'll appreciate while you turn on a wet bridge, claw around an off-camber sweeper, or haul the mail through a slippery berm. Bonus: The extra pedal clearance lets you get on the gas sooner . . . braaap!

Another Reason to Be Light and Strong

When you're pulling 2 g's through a big berm, it's twice as hard as normal to maintain your position and lift your legs for each pedal stroke. The lighter and stronger you are, the better you can cope with your awesome cornering forces.

Brian railed this berm so hard he tore out a swath of dirt. His position above the bike allowed him to maintain control when the tires broke loose.

Leading with your upper body lessens your bike lean and leaves more tire on the ground.

The Truth About Countersteering

Contrary to popular belief, countersteering is not turning your wheel the opposite way while you skid around a turn, nor is it riding in circles on your kitchen counter. Countersteering uses gyroscopic forces and the geometry of your bike to lean you into a corner. High speeds require it. Here's how to countersteer into a fast left turn:

- ○ Turn your wheel slightly to the *right*. For a brief instant, the bike will steer right.

- ○ The bike will almost immediately lean to the left. As soon as the bike leans, you'll begin to turn left.

- ○ Because of the way steering geometry works, the wheel will flop over to the left and help you make your turn. Voilà, you're turning left.

- ○ The bike will hold its lean angle without any input from you. Try loosening your grip on the bars. See? You're still carving. For more lean, nudge your bars to the right. For less lean, nudge 'em to the left. Be sure to let the wheel flop where it wants to. Try this in high-speed turns. You'll be stoked.

Countersteering into a left turn

You need speed.

1. Turn bars slightly to the right.

2. Bike will lean to the left.

3. Relax. The bars will turn to the left. You're carving!

The Motorcycle Safety Foundation teaches its students to push left to go left. As you lean your body into a left turn, press forward on your left handlebar. The countersteer and lean will complement each other, and you'll soon be railing like a pro bikercrosser.

Pedals Planted or Level?

Outside Pedal Down

For long turns.

For flat and off-camber turns.

Any time you need to set a hard edge.

> Note: Never turn with your inside pedal down, unless you're going like 0.1 miles per hour.

Pedals Level

Short, quick turns. (It takes too long to switch from side to side.) Besides, you want to pump these turns.

Rough ground. You don't want your outside pedal digging into roots and such. Trust us.

Inside Foot In or Out?

A dropped foot can help you through long, sketchy corners. Leave your outside foot on the pedal and plant your butt on the seat. Take your inside foot and skim it along the ground. This lowers your center of gravity a bit, and it puts more weight on your rear tire. Your rear suspension works under your mass, and your bike tracks like crazy. Even if it isn't helping all that much, you feel safer with your foot out, don't you?

You might compromise your first pedal strokes, but if you carry mega speed through the corner, who cares?

Greg Minnaar finds traction where there is none in his qualifying run at the 2004 Big Bear national downhill.

Rail Berms

Berm
Positive camber; bank

Berms intimidate many mountain bikers who didn't grow up on BMX tracks, but they provide the ultimate turning experience. The Sea Otter Classic slalom course has some of the best berms ever. You blast down the start ramp, finesse a couple grassy gates, hammer straight down the fall line, and fall into this huge 100-degree left. You pull so many g's it feels like the flesh is melting off your face. You get a few pedal strokes on the way out and then—pow!—you hit a triple jump and rail through a perfect 180. If you ride that course, you will smile for the rest of your life.

You don't need race-sculpted berms to enjoy the benefits of positive camber. Look for worn lines, ruts, little banks—anything you can press your tires against. A smooth, nicely arced berm practically rides itself.

Lay off the brakes.   You can carry more speed through a berm than any other kind of turn. As a matter of fact, if the banking is steep enough, you can safely go faster than your brain will let you.

Lean it like you mean it.   Steep berms allow deep lean angles. For every berm, there is a "perfect" speed at which your lean angle presses your tires directly into the ground (see the chart on page 60). For example, a turn with a 15-foot radius and a 45-degree bank would be perfect at 15 miles per hour. With this perfect lean, you don't even need tire traction; you could run Teflon and still rail the corner. When you go so fast that your lean exceeds the berm's banking, you have to make up the traction difference as if it's a flat turn. You usually end up leaning your bike more than your body.

The steepness and traction in this berm let Brian rail directly over his wheels.

Brian goes way "too fast" for this berm. He leans his bike and weights the outside pedal to maintain traction.

Go as high as you need to.   Most berms are flattest at the bottom and steepest at the top. Try to match your lean angle with the banking. If you're going slow, ride low. If you're going fast, ride high. Bonus tip: The fastest riders create a narrow, overhanging track along the top of a berm. If you have enough speed to ride that line, you'll rail like a Hot Wheels car. The berms at the Encinitas YMCA were over vertical. You could ride them as fast as you wanted. Heck, it seemed like you couldn't ride them fast enough.

Keep pedaling!   This can be hard to fathom, but if the berm isn't too rough, you can sit and pedal the whole way. French downhill legend Nico Vouilloz did that all the time.

Mind your lines.   In a perfect, constant berm, you don't need to worry about early, middle, or late apexes. Just follow the bank around the turn. That said, you can exit fast by squaring the turn high near the beginning of the turn and then accelerating down toward the exit (see the passing section in chapter 11, page 164). Definitely take a critical look at your berm. If it's high on the entrance and low on the exit, enter it high and drop down on the way out. If it's low on the entrance and high on the exit, enter it low and let your speed carry you up the bank.

Brian Rails Like a Roller Coaster

At the 1994 World Cup slalom in Vail, Colorado, the course had these super-steep, killer berms. They were almost vertical. It felt like I was going through on a roller coaster, like I was on rails. It was like you couldn't go fast enough. If I could have carried another 10 miles per hour into those turns, I'd have done it. When a berm is that steep, you get so much traction you need high pressure just so you don't roll your tires off the rim. Yeah, when you blast into a sweet 90- or 180-degree berm, you better have some psi's in those tires.

Carve Flat Turns

Flat turn
Zero camber

A Hot Wheels car can rail a berm. Flat turns require skill. Tires scraping across the ground like to slide, and they require finesse to stay on track.

Run great tires.   In the middle of a slippery turn, the difference between a $20 and a $50 handlebar means nothing. The difference between a $20 and a $50 tire means everything. The right size, casing, pattern, and compound provide more traction, which is important. What's even more important is your confidence. Believe in your tires, believe in yourself.

Lean your bike more than your body.   Weight that outside pedal while you're at it.

Load it.   As you initiate a tight turn or square off a wide turn, unweight your bike and then cram your tires into the ground.

Most flat turns aren't entirely flat.   Look for a rut, a tire track, or anything you can use as a mini-berm.

Jon Watt rails this flat turn as if it has a berm. The keys: (1) good tires, (2) leaned bike, and (3) eyes forward.

Survive Off-Camber Turns

Everything that applies to flat turns applies to off-camber turns, only more so. When you combine your positive lean with the ground's negative lean, you get a traction nightmare.

Off camber
Negative camber

Go slow.   With the ground pointing away from your tires, a skid is closer than ever.

Do a late apex.   Hit the apex very high and let yourself drift lower as you exit. If you expect the drift, it won't be so scary. A rut or berm frequently forms on the exit, where your predecessors finally caught traction. Use it!

Get even lower, stay even looser, and look even farther ahead than in flat turns.   The sketchiness will tempt you to tighten up. You must resist. You are a corner-carving machine. Make it happen, baby!

Try to turn where it's not actually off camber.   Look for any flat or, even better, banked surface where you can square off the turn.

Steve Peat weights his outside pedal and follows a tiny rut around this deal-breaker on the 2004 Big Bear national downhill course.

Default switchback lines

Downhill

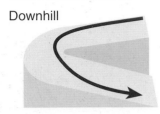

Uphill

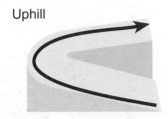

Conquer Switchbacks

Switchbacks' sharpness, steepness, and exposure turn flowy riders into wigged-out stickmen. But remember: Switchbacks are nothing more than tight, steep corners.

Slow WAY down for downhill switchbacks.   As you drop through the turn, you want to reach a happy speed, not scare yourself into an unfortunate braking incident.

You almost always want a late apex.   For a downhill left switchback, slow down, enter to the far right, square the turn, and drop through to the exit. Early apexes can be deadly—that outside exit line tends to be a cliff.

Use the ruts.   When a rain channel cruises around the outside of a wide switchback, rail it just like a berm. When the rut carves a tight line across the inside, drop your rear tire into the rut and track your brakeless front tire around the outside of it. When the rut runs around the outside of a tight switchback, let your rear tire follow it and steer to the inside. A little rear brake keeps your rear meat in the track (only on closed courses, of course).

Smart riders enter ultra wide over the rock and rail around the far outside. Most people enter to the inside, and they fail to make the corner.

Pull out a foot.   Sometimes it pays to drop your inside foot and whip your bike around a super-tight corner. Steep exits bring you right back up to speed. In flat exits, you'll lose some time finding your pedal. The San Juan Trail in southern California has dozens of steep switchbacks. When we follow people down and they pull their feet into the turns, they might gap us a little, but we're back on their tails within two strokes.

Nose-wheelie!   On a slow, tight switchback with decent traction, you can do a nose wheelie and kick the back end around. You don't have to swing it the full 180 degrees; you need just enough to help aim you into the turn.

Climbing switchbacks.   Switchbacks only occur on steep hills. Follow the widest line possible to reduce the grade and give your rear tire room to track inward. Build momentum with a couple hard cranks, and keep the power going as you round the bend. Hold your bike upright and lean your body into the turn. If you can't pedal because of ruts or roots, make sure you gain tons of speed on the entrance. Don't brake!

Skid Into Loose Corners

Don't skid on public trails. Use these techniques only on racecourses— and then only sparingly. If you can rail a corner without skidding, that's usually fastest. Basically, if a turn has a berm, rail it. If there's enough traction or space for you to carry momentum through a turn, then carve it. Skidding only makes sense in slow, slippery corners that you want to square off. Use the skid to aim your bike in a new direction, and then resume your rolling.

As you zoom down the right lane of a gravelly doubletrack, a flat left turn approaches. If you arc through the inside of the turn, your front tire will surely wash out. The solution: a skid setup. Remember: This is about steering, not slowing down. Bring your bike to a reasonable speed before you reach the corner.

1. Nail the rear brake to break the tire loose. Note how far outside the main line Peaty chose to begin his turn.

2. Get the bike skidding sideways (note the lean).

3. Lean forward and steer with your front tire. Do not touch the front brake. You need your front tire to pull you into the corner.

4. When the rear end swings around to where you want it, release the brake. Your rear tire will catch and you'll shoot into the corner. Sa-weet!

This loose, off-camber right demands one of Steve Peat's patented skid setups.

Rear-Brake Drag

With dual suspension, you can lightly drag your rear brake through rough berms. This keeps the rear end in contact with the ground and squats the rear end down, which helps the bike track better. Give it a try.

Be ready for your tires to slip. If the traction was good, you wouldn't be doing a skid setup, would you? When the skid happens, stay off the brakes and steer where you want to go.

Other fun stuff:

- Try a little kickout to help set up the skid.
- You can skid into the beginning of a corner and then release the brakes and rail the rest of it.
- You can kind of half-skid, half-carve when you're going fast.
- Controlled skidding is tricky. Practice in a safe place. Use flat pedals.

Pump Berms for Free Speed

When you encounter a tight turn with a steep bank and an abrupt transition, you can pump it as if it's the landing of a jump (see "Pump Rhythms," page 112). When you think about it, a berm is basically a hole on its side. For extra speed and traction, try dropping into the turn, pumping the transition, then getting light on the exit. When you feel the bike unweight, that's your cue to start pedaling and set up for the next turn.

Pumping a berm A good pump will maintain or even increase your speed.

1. Drop your weight as low as possible into the berm.

2. At the transitional point, push hard with your arms and legs.

Deal With Drift

Mountain bike tires slip. They squirm. They drift. They skid. They skip.

When you haul ass on persnickety surfaces, that's what happens. You'd think we'd be used to it, but most of us freak out when traction runs out and the tires get loose. It doesn't take many cliff drops and cases of poison oak to develop a case of drift phobia.

No matter how boffo your braking, how luscious your lines, how potent your pump, you will eventually drift in a turn. The good news is, you don't have to be afraid. You see, your tires *never* grab the ground completely. Any time you ride around a curve, the rubber alternately grips and slips. On pavement, the knobs might squirm one millimeter every tenth of a second. You don't even notice that. On sand over hardpack, they might slip an inch every second. No biggie. On embedded rocks, they might skip a foot every few seconds. Umm . . . yikes! While a front-wheel side trip feels wild, remember that as long as you stay loose and let the bike do its thing, your tire will regain traction, and you'll continue through the corner. Whether this happens 10 times per second or once per minute makes little difference.

Grip-slip-grip is natural. Get used to it. Be ready for it.

Scrutinize the corner.   If you see gravel or marbles, don't be surprised when things get jiggy. Same with speed. Hauling the mail into a flat or off-camber turn is just asking for funny business.

Aim for a tighter line than you need.   This gives you room to drift. You can always open up your turn, but tightening will make you crash. Bonus: You're probably not the first person to slide through this corner. There might be a bank—or at least a pile of dust—where everyone else finally caught traction. Use it.

Lean your bike and keep your weight over the contact patch.   This literally keeps you on top of the situation. Breaking loose while you're leaned far inside is like kicking the bottom of an upturned broom.

Balance the slippage.   You want both wheels to go together (this is that two-wheel drift you always hear about). If one wheel starts to slide more than the other, subtly shift your weight to that wheel. When you maintain a long drift, it feels like your bike is walking sideways.

If you're turning right and your front wheel suddenly lets go, steer with the slide (to the left) until it catches, then gently turn the wheel back to the right.

If the rear lets go, keep your weight on the front tire. As long as your front is tracking, it'll pull the rear into line.

Stay loose.   Yes, for the ten-thousandth time. The more you fight the slide, the more you'll slide and the dorkier you'll look. Your bike must be free to find its way. After some practice, gravelly corners will feel as predictable as pavement.

Rally Slide

Here's a little trick for ya: Say you want to slide into a left turn. Skid your rear tire to the left (toward the inside of the turn), then whip it around to the right and enter the turn. This left-right swing adds more energy to your entrance.

When the going gets loose, hold your line and trust that your tires will hook up—eventually.

Drill Your Drift

Find a flat, slippery corner with a consistent, nonfatal surface and nothing big to run into. Gravel on hardpack is good; sand on hardpack is better. Run pads and flat pedals. Enter the corner at ludicrous speed. Experiment with different body positions to see which tire goes first. Lose your front tire and then find it. Lose your rear tire and then find it. Then strive for that happy medium, "walking" your bike sideways through the corner. Yee-haw!

Shoot Your Troubles

Problem: You feel yourself falling to the inside of a turn. Heck, you might actually hit the deck.

Solution: You're leaning too much for your speed and the tightness of the turn. Lean less. (Duh.)

Problem: You blast straight through the turn. You might feel yourself tensing up and hitting the brakes as you follow a tangent into a Joshua tree.

Solutions: Most of the time, merely leaning more will do the trick. Just pitch your bike into the corner, and it'll probably come around. If that doesn't work for ya, try slowing down and following a gentler arc. Also, always, always, *always* look where you want to go, out past the exit of the turn.

Problem: Your rear end slides out.

Solutions: Enter the turn with your weight a little farther back. When the rear tire goes, lean forward to keep the front tire tracking. If you sit back, you'll keep sliding out until you're looking back up the trail—"hey dudes, check me out!"

Problem: Your front wheel washes out.

Solutions: Enter the turn with your weight farther forward. When your front tire starts to go, let it. Steer in the direction it slides until it starts to track again, then turn back to where you want to go. This whole mess can happen in a fraction of a second. When your front tire goes all at once, slap a foot down for stability and try to pull the bike back underneath you.

Wire a Corner

Here's a fun drill: Pick a corner that gives you a hard time. Try entering faster and faster until you can't make it. Try all sorts of tricks. Lean differently. Weight your outside pedal. Drop your inside foot. Load your bike. Figure out what works best, and then take it to the big show!

Problem: You have trouble making flat and off-camber turns.

Solutions: Lean your bike more and weight the outside pedal. Pick smoother lines. Load your tires for temporary extra traction.

Problem: In berms, you find yourself steering up the banks to stay on course.

Solution: You're going too slow! Either speed up or ride lower in the berm, where it isn't so steep.

Problem: You freak out whenever your tires break loose.

Solution: Either slow down so you don't drift or practice drifting in a controlled situation. This is a natural part of mountain biking; we suggest you get used to it!

Corners have the most variation in mountain biking. The possible combinations of radius, camber, elevation, surface, speed, and lines stagger the imagination. Corners separate world-class trails from merely fun trails and great riders from merely good riders. When you can pick great lines, carry the right speed, and maximize your traction, you'll rip on the best trails the world has to offer.

6

Wheelie and Hop Over Anything

If we lived in a two-dimensional world, we could get along fine without lifting our wheels off the ground. But riding in a two-dimensional world would be awfully flat, wouldn't it?

Mountain biking is all about that vertical dimension. Ripples, roots, rocks, ravines: They force us to go over or around. If you can't lift your bike, you're stuck going around. That's entertaining, but the real thrills begin when you can take the bird line: straight over.

Notes to beginners: Learn these moves step by step—first the wheelie, then the rear wheel lift, and then the bunny hop. Start with small obstacles on forgiving ground. Wear your helmet, gloves, and pads.

Lift That Front Wheel

Boys learn to lift their front wheel around the time they learn their ABCs. They goof around in front of their homes, tugging and tugging until—voilà—they've popped their very first wheelie.

We have no idea what the girls were doing at this time (our wives were hanging with Barbie), but most of them missed the wheelie lesson. So you end up with these excellent women who can arrange million-dollar deals and rail singletrack, but who can't pop wheelies for the life of them. They are strong and free, but any curb stops them in their tracks. When we began this book, our wives fell into this category. We have no doubt that if they took the time to learn, they'd both become wheelie-popping queens.

Traditional wisdom says most women aren't strong enough to lift their bikes. Bah-hooey to that. Ninety-eight pound boys routinely manual 40-pound downhill bikes, and plenty of women are stronger than them.

You wheel-on-the-grounders might be asking why you need to pop wheelies. The reasons outnumber the shoes in our wives' closets: jagged rocks deflect your wheel, bumps slow you down, and curbs thwart shopping trips, to name a few. When you can lift your front wheel over obstacles, you retain speed and control in all sorts of situations.

Sitting and Pedaling Wheelie

You're climbing a nice singletrack with excellent traction. A three-inch root crosses the trail. Bashing into it will slow you down or knock you off line. If you can get your front wheel over that bugger and keep pedaling, your rear tire will crawl right over it.

GET YOUR WHEEL OFF THE GROUND

1. Start in a neutral position.
2. Crouch down and forward, with your bum on the saddle. Your power pedal should be at around 2 o'clock.

1. Neutral position. 2. Crouch forward. 3. Crank and push yourself back. 4. Keep leaning and pedaling.

Center of gravity

3. Explosively push your torso upward and backward with your arms. At the same time, uncork a powerful pedal stroke. If you are nice to puppies, your front wheel will pop up.

4. Keep your arms straight and your weight back. Keep pedaling.

KEEP IT THERE

Pedaling around with your wheel in the air isn't very useful on the trail, but it looks cool. Learn to balance sitting wheelies before you move up to coaster wheelies.

Keep lifting your front wheel until you find the balancing point. The magic spot will feel weightless, like you are neither working to keep the wheel up nor falling on your bum. It's all about getting comfortable with the balance. Here are some tricks to help you stay on top:

Find the balance.   Once you get to the magic spot, keep pedaling nice and easy. If you feel yourself falling forward, pedal harder. If you feel yourself falling backward, brake a little. If you start falling to one side, lean to the other side.

Choose the right gear.   A really low gear gives you a fast pop but short loft time. A higher gear gives you less pop but longer loft. Find your happy medium. When your kung fu is good, you'll use your normal, low climbing gear. You can get it spinning very easily, for great explosion, and you keep it spinning to maintain lift.

Pedal all the way up to it.   It's easiest to approach your wheelie point already pedaling and then give it some extra juice when the time is right. After you get the hang of this, you can try jabbing the pedals from a coast. Warning: The lift is a bit more violent, and low-quality rear hubs tend to hesitate before they grab (and they might skip under your awesome power).

Never stop pedaling.   Keep turning the pedals after you pop your wheel up. It's easier to give a little more or less gas if your foot's already on the pedal.

Light brakes.   If you jab your rear brake, your front wheel will slam to the ground so fast you won't be able to stop it. All you need is a tiny bit of lever pressure. If you find you keep giving it too much brake at once, try lightly dragging the brake as you ride. This is like your constant pedaling: It's easier to give a bit more or less when you're already giving some.

Setup Tip

Lower your seat.

Stay loose.   We can't say this enough. Sit lightly on the saddle so you can slide forward or back, right or left. Feel free to sway your knees in and out. If you're using flat pedals, you can tilt your foot to the side or even hang it out like an outrigger.

Coasting Wheelie, aka "Manual"

When you're coasting downhill or on flat ground, this is the best way to get your front wheel over trouble. You'd be amazed at what your rear wheel can roll over after your front is already clear, especially with suspension. Remember to stay loose and keep your speed reasonable.

1. Neutral position.   2. Crouch forward.   3. Torso back, feet forward.   4. Keep leaning and pulling.

GET YOUR WHEEL OFF THE GROUND

1. Start in a neutral position, arms and legs slightly bent, weight centered.

2. Crouch down and forward. Bring your chest close to your handlebars.

3. All of a sudden, with great vigor, push your torso upward and backward. Straighten your arms all the way. Straighten your legs a bit and push your hips backward and your pedals forward. Imagine your body rotating back over the contact patch of your rear tire.

4. Let your body continue to rotate up and back. When your arms straighten, your body's momentum will pull the front end up. (This way, you lift the bike with the mass of your body rather than your puny little arms.) The farther back you go, the closer your center of gravity gets to your rear tire's contact patch, and the longer you can keep your wheel up. Don't go too far, though, or you'll "loop out," which means "fall on your bum."

If you can get your front wheel onto a sidewalk, you can let your rear wheel bash right over the curb. Go slow and stay loose, and soon you'll experience real freedom.

KEEP IT THERE

Because you can't use your pedals to cheat your front end upward, you have to maintain balance with perfect body position and sharp reflexes. Expert manualers can balance forever over all sorts of terrain, from rocks to bumps to stream crossings.

Here are some tips to help you find some balance in your life:

○ Straighten your arms and lean all the way back to the balance point.

○ If you need to raise your front wheel, push your hips backward or pedals forward.

○ If you need to lower your front wheel, pull yourself forward.

○ It's all in the hips. Leave your arms pretty much straight.

MANUAL TIPS

Preload.   When you go from your neutral position to your crouch, drop your weight quickly and then immediately push back upward. The rebound of your bike's tires, frame, and suspension will add to your explosion.

Timing.   You want your wheel to be highest when it reaches the obstacle. Lift too soon and you hit on the upswing. Too late and you hit on the downfall. Perfect timing depends on your speed, the height of the obstacle, and how fast you lift your wheel. Pop lots of wheelies, and perfect timing will come.

Learn on a hardtail.   On a full-suspension bike, you not only have to maintain your balance over the rear wheel, you also have to compensate for the moving suspension.

Problem:
Front wheel too low.

Solution:
Move hips backward.

Manual a Double

It's easier to manual across a pair of humps than to manual on flat ground. The first hump helps lift your front wheel, and the second hump gives you a target to aim for. This little trick gives you a feel for manual balance, plus it's a fast way to get over the humps.

1. Let the first hump lift your front wheel. Shift your weight backward to keep the front end up.

2. Bend your legs as your wheel rolls up the hump.

3. Push your rear wheel down the backside. This gives you some free speed and helps hold the front end up.

4. Set the front tire onto the backside of the second hump.

5. Absorb the hump with your legs.

6. Straighten your legs and pump down the backside.

As your skills improve, manual all the way over the second hump. This will give you a better pump and elevate you one step closer to manualing greatness. The front side of a tabletop makes a nice manualing aid, as well.

Wheelie Sideways

An hour into your singletrack climb, you enter a super-tight switchback. You know your bike won't track through the deep rut carving through the apex, so you ride past it, pick your wheel up, swing your bike around, and set your wheel down at the top of the turn.

1. Look and lean into the turn like normal.
2. Explode with power and pick up the front end. Burst forward out of your saddle. Push with your legs and pull with your arms. Keep leaning into the turn!
3. Set it back down and enjoy the rest of your ride.

Lift Your Rear Wheel

To get over big, sharp rocks and impress everyone on Rodeo Drive, you gotta give your rear end a lift.

1. Crouch and lean back.

2. Lunge upward and forward.

3. Let it come up.

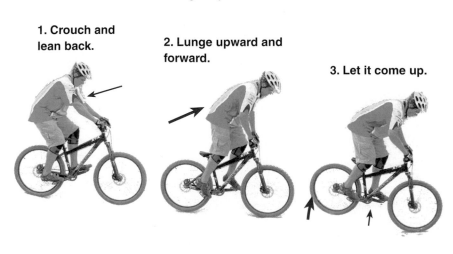

Basic Rear-Wheel Lift

1. Crouch and lean back.
2. Lunge upward and forward. Really snap against your pedals. This is where most of the lifting force comes from.
3. Let it come up. Lighten your feet to let the pedals rise. As your body comes forward, twist your wrists and push your bars forward.

Exaggerate.   This is all about weighting and unweighting. While you're learning, lean all the way back, then hurl yourself all the way forward. Make it count.

Cheat (if you need to).   With clip-in pedals, you can easily pull the rear wheel upward. This is fine and good (if you're a sissy), but it's best to learn without relying on clip-ins. Flat pedals will teach you better form, and you'll be able to hop higher in the long run.

Kick It Out

In a kickout, you keep your front wheel on the ground and hop your rear wheel sideways. This trick was a big deal in the first grade, and it remains useful.

Kick your rear wheel out to avoid a rock in a turn. Do a kickout as you enter a flat, fast turn; when you set your rear tire down, it catches traction and shoots you into the corner. Neat.

If you can lift your rear wheel straight up, a kickout is easy. Say you want to kick out to the left:

1. Steer and lean to the left. Keep your hips to the right of the saddle, with your weight a bit to the rear.

2. Lunge forward and to the left. Your hips should swing to the other side of your bike.

3. The bike will follow. Note these are flat pedals. The pop comes from the rapid load and unload, not from pulling with your feet.

4. Take that, Mr. Bottle!

One wheel at a time: How to slowly hop over a small obstacle

1. Load the spring. As you approach, crouch down and forward.

2. Lift the front wheel. Quickly push your torso away from the bike and pull on the bars with straight arms. (See the wheelie section.)

3. Lunge forward. As soon as your front wheel lands, push explosively on your pedals, then slightly unweight your feet to let the pedals come up.

4. Lift your rear wheel. As your body continues to lunge forward, push the bars forward as well. You are rotating the bike on the front contact patch.

5. Touchdown. Rock and roll. You did it!

Get Over Small Obstacles

When an obstacle fits below your chainrings, you can slowly cross it by lifting first your front and then your back wheel over it. Use this technique while you ride slowly over any small object: a branch, a rock, and even the dreaded curb. Let's use a couple of two-by-fours as an example:

1. Load the spring. As you approach the lumber, crouch down and forward.

2. Lift the front wheel. Immediately push your torso away from the bike and pull the bars as you lean back (see the wheelie section on page 76).

3. Lunge forward. As soon as your front wheel touches down, push explosively into your pedals and propel your body forward. After you push, lighten your feet to allow the pedals to come up. If you're clipped in, you can actually pull the bike upward, but that's cheating.

4. Air that rear wheel. As your body continues to lunge forward, push the bars forward as well. Think about rotating the bike around your front wheel.

5. Absorb the landing. You did it!

Hop Over Large Obstacles

If the obstacle is too big to fit beneath your chainrings, you have to lift both wheels together. This is a bona fide bunny hop. When you can hop over an obstacle without slowing your flow, you'll enjoy a whole new level of fun and freedom. Logs won't stop you. Rocks will make you smile. Curbs . . . ha!

1. Load the spring. **2. Lift your front wheel.** **3. Lift your rear wheel.** **4. Have a good attitude.** **5. Smooth landing.**

1. Load the spring. Crouch down and forward. Bring your chest close to your handlebars. The faster you compress, the more rebound you'll get for your hop.

2. Lift your front wheel. Shift your weight backward and get your front end up (review the coasting manual, page 78).

3. Lift the rear wheel. Timing is essential here. At the moment your weight presses into your rear wheel, push explosively down into the pedals and spring upward. The bike feels like it's springing out from under you. If you get light on your pedals, and you live a righteous life, your rear wheel will levitate.

4. Have a good attitude. Let your bike arc through the air. It should be level as you cross the obstacle.

5. Smooth landing. For small and medium hops over pine trunks, let your front wheel land first. Absorb the landing with your arms, then your legs. For huge hops over park benches, land rear wheel first (for more on drops, see chapter 7, "Drop Like a Feather").

When low speed won't let you clear the obstacle, let your wheels bop the top. Here are some assorted bunny hopping tips:

Timing. The faster you're going, the sooner you should start your hop. If you take off too late, your rear wheel will clip the log on its way up, and then you're in for a bucking good time.

Suspension. A suspension bike takes longer to load and unload, so you have to begin your hop earlier and time your compression and releases more slowly than with a hardtail. The same hop requires more effort with suspension than without.

Pedals. Clip-in pedals let you easily pull your bike up with your feet. We recommend you learn to hop the real way—with flat pedals. When you hop with flats, use your forearms to rotate the bars forward and help get the rear end up.

Curbs and ledges. If you're going fast enough to clear the top, try to land with your wheels level. The landing will be close to the peak of your hop, and you'll land extra smoothly. If you're going too slowly for that maneuver, go for some lunge action (see "Lunge Onto a Ledge" later in this chapter).

Hop Sideways

You're hauling the mail down an eroded doubletrack, and a deep rain rut crosses your line. No problem: Do one of your sweet high-speed bunny hops, with a twist. This trick is also handy for hopping from the street onto a sidewalk, or over a random wooden plank.

1. Just before your hop, steer and lean in the direction you're heading.
2. Hop like a maniac. With your body in the air, swing your bike to the other side.
3. Straighten your front wheel and set your bike down. Since you'll be turning as you land, lean a bit to the inside.

Hop in Place

Here's another cute trick. Hop up and down a few inches, and make constant little corrections as if you're on a pogo stick. When you get the hang of this, you can hop forward, backward, side to side, and even in a different direction.

○ Do it anywhere to practice your balance.

○ On the trail, it gives you time to check things out and hop over to a new line if you need to. If you overshoot a switchback turn, you can stop, hop a 180, and continue on your merry way.

Lunge Onto a Ledge

You follow the white dots up a slickrock face in Moab, Utah. The traction is incredible, so you have no excuse to get off and walk. You reach a foot-high ledge. Your buddy just seems to lunge up and over the thing. Here's how you can do the same. For those of you who live in soggier climes, feel free to lunge over rocks, roots, and water bars.

This move is easiest when you can pedal the whole way. If the rise is so sharp you'll stab a pedal, you have two choices: (1) time your pedaling so you arrive with pedals level or (2) give it a burst of speed and coast—you'll have to lunge much harder (step 5) without the added pedal oomph.

Uphill lunge   Note how the head and torso stay level, and the bike comes up to the rider.

6. Back to neutral position and on the gas!

5. Push forward with arms; push and absorb with legs.

4. Pull wheel to top and move body forward to balance point.

3. Power stroke and spring backward to lift front end.

2. Crouch forward.

1. Neutral position; weight centered.

1. Approach in your patented neutral position, eyes tracking beyond the obstacle.

2. Crouch forward to compress your suspension fork.

3. Give it a sharp power stroke and spring backward to lift the front end. This is unlike a manual in that you don't want to balance on the rear wheel. Your weight will be centered only about three-quarters of the way back. As you rotate backward, keep pedaling and pull with your arms.

4. Pull with your arms to set your front wheel on the obstacle. As you set down, move forward to re-center your weight.

5. As the rear wheel reaches the obstacle, give it another surge of power and snap downward with your legs. When the rear end upweights, push forward with your arms and legs. The bike will pass between your legs, and you'll find yourself behind the saddle.

6. When you get clear, resume your neutral position, keep your eyes forward, and get ready for whatever's next.

Pedal Hop

Say you need to cross a deep gully, but you're going too slowly to hop across it and there isn't enough space to pedal up to speed. It's time for the pedal hop, a trials move with trail appeal. This is also a handy urban move.

As always, you need to be in the perfect gear—not too hard and not too easy.

1. Approach low and forward. Time your power pedal so it tops out at the edge of the gap.

2. Explode up and forward. Push the pedals and pull the bars. Drive your hips all the way forward. Hello, Mr. Stem.

3. Push your bike in front of you. This will give you extra distance.

4. Suck it up.

If you accelerate fast enough and pull hard enough, your rear wheel will launch you like a rocket.

Shoot Your Troubles

Problem: When you try to lift your front wheel, it only pops up for an instant, even when you yank as hard as you can.

Solution: Sharply push your weight backward and pull on the bars with straight arms. You don't lift your front end with your arms; you lift it with your body mass. At low speeds, snap your pedals to help get the front end up. Keep your finger on the rear brake lever in case you start to loop out.

Problem: Your rear wheel seems stuck to the ground. All the grunting and groaning in the world won't lift it.

Solution: Load and unload your pedals very sharply. Really shift your weight forward. If you're running clips, go ahead and pull your pedals up (cheating!). You can also tap your front brake to help raise your rear end. You can swing your rear end around to help you set up for tight turns.

Problem: When you try to bunny hop, your rear wheel doesn't fly as high as your front.

Solution: Master the basic rear-wheel lift before you step up to hops. Really accentuate the one-two, front-rear timing. Push and pull on your bars and then load and unload your pedals.

You wouldn't enter an archery contest without arrows, and it's just as silly to ride trails without knowing how to wheelie and hop. These "get-over-stuff" skills are some of the most important in your quiver: When a log appears on the trail, whip out a bunny hop. When you hurtle into a rock garden, bust into a manual. As you race through a rhythm section, hop the first roller, manual the next two, and jump the last three. Heck, you never know which arrow you'll need.

7

Drop Like a Feather

© Photo-John

Y ou're flying down the A-Line trail at the Whistler Mountain Bike Park in British Columbia on your little slalom bike. The trail has a sweet rhythm: left, jump, right, jump, left, jump, right, jump. Up ahead, a few riders stand on the trail, looking down. Oh, yeah, you remember, it's that big rock drop. You slow down, cut to the right side, and take off. The crushing gravel and pounding bumps disappear in a rush of wind and weightlessness. You fall, fall, fall to a little downslope, land with a squish, and set up for the next left. Aah . . . good living on the front line of the mountain bike revolution.

Dropoffs have been part of mountain biking since the beginning, but today's trails and riding styles incorporate more and bigger drops than ever. Normal riders take vertical lines on cross-country trails, stunts are popping up everywhere, and madmen huck off 50-foot cliffs. When you learn to take off safely and land smoothly, you'll have more freedom and fun anywhere.

Land Smoothly

So you can bottom your nine-inch freeride bike off a curb? Don't be too proud of yourself. Smooth landings are where it's at. Save your body, save your bike, save the world.

Minimize the drop. If you're just out riding, find a line that drops less and aims you downward toward the landing instead of flipping you skyward. When you reach your takeoff, crouch your body as low as possible so your body doesn't have to fall as far. Get your bike back on the ground as soon and as smoothly as possible. There's nothing cool about breaking bottom-bracket spindles and ankle bones.

Keep your front end up until your rear takes off. Dropping one wheel at a time is dangerous business: If your chainring catches the lip, you pitch forward. If your front wheel falls into the landing crater, you flop over the bars. If your rear rolls forward while your front drops straight down, you become a human catapult. The bottom line: Until you're completely airborne, keep your front wheel level with or above your rear wheel. Word.

High-Speed Drop Action

At the 1999 Sea Otter Classic dual slalom, the top guys (Brian included) hauled over a three-foot drop, pushed their rear wheels down, and started pedaling with their front wheels still in the air. These guys got max smoothness plus max speed—and it looked rad!

Use speed to your advantage. The faster you go, the more easily you keep your front end up until your rear end drops. If you go fast enough, you hardly have to do anything to match your bike's attitude to that of the trail. Speed lets you clear gnarly rocks and bad landings. Flat landings feel smoother when you land with momentum than when you land slowly and stick to the ground.

Match your landing to the slope. On flat landings, get your rear wheel down first. This minimizes your free fall and lets you absorb the landing with your legs. On downhill landings, get your front wheel down first. Steep landings are so smooth you'll wonder when you're going to land. If you do land rear wheel first on a downslope, your front end will slam down, and you'll be bummed.

Big is cool, but don't be a fool. If the drop is lower than your knee pads, you can usually roll right off it, no big deal. But when drops grow taller than your wheels, you gotta start paying attention to your form, and you should definitely look before you leap. As Mr. T would say, "Don't jack the height until you're droppin' right."

Fast Drop to Downhill

Whether you know it or not, you probably do drops all the time. You might not session 20-foot cliffs, but as you fly down trails, you spend a lot of time out of contact with the ground: You haul over holes, blip beyond boulders, and soar beyond slopes. Really, a "drop" happens any time you carry enough speed to arc above the ground.

The art of dropping is the art of controlling your bike in the air and landing smoothly. When you master this art, you can hop over objects at speed, skip rough sections, and maintain momentum when the ground drops out from beneath you. By the way, a drop is basically the second half of a jump. When you can land smoothly from a takeoff, you're ready to propel yourself skyward.

Cool. When you encounter drops on your favorite trail (or cliff), try not to jump upward. Stay low and rely on speed. The faster you go, the easier this is.

Bike Setup Tip

If you want to stick landings like Wade Simmons and Richie Schley, stiffen your springs and slow your rebound.

Fast drop to downslope   While this might look scary from the ladder, a little confidence and speed makes it feel easy.

2. Push bike forward and get your body back.

1. Crouch in forward position.

3. Drop your front end to match the landing angle.

4. Suck it up, front wheel first.

1. Crouch as you approach the takeoff.

2. As your front wheel leaves the lip, push your hips back and snap forward with your feet. This accelerates the bike forward and gives your front wheel a little lift. It also moves you toward the back of your bike.

3. Match the angle of your bike to the angle of the landing.

4. Land front wheel first or with both wheels at the same time. A pronounced rear-wheel landing will slam the front to the ground. Ouch.

Dropping into a turn.   Steep trails frequently drop over outcroppings and then fold directly into tight, rutted turns. Any time you drop directly into a turn, take the drop as you normally would, then immediately center your weight so you can corner well. If you hit the turn with your weight still in the back seat, your front tire will wash out.

Slow Drop to Flat

Dropping off a rock, ladder, or loading dock at low speed is actually a lot harder than soaring off an outcropping at Mach 5. This move is both old-school trials and new-school North Shore. It requires you to lift your front wheel and keep it there, and then absorb a blunt landing.

Practice on a low curb from a standstill. As you get the hang of controlling your bike's attitude, step it up a little at a time. You want to avoid the thing where your front wheel falls to the ground and your rear wheel or chainring tags the edge of the drop, sending you over the bars for certain.

Use this approach any time you don't have enough speed to quickly clear the takeoff. The more slowly you go, the more you have to pop your front tire up and accelerate to keep it up.

1. Crouch as you approach the takeoff.

2. As you reach the edge, push your body back and jab your power pedal. Try to time it so your pedal is at 12 o'clock. Be in a gear that gives you good pop. Pedal softly as you approach. If you need to, ratchet your pedal to get it in the right position.

3. Keep accelerating until your rear wheel takes off. Don't let your front end drop!

4. As soon as your rear takes off, push the back of the bike down.

5. When the rear touches down, begin absorbing the impact with your legs.

6. When the front lands, do the same with your arms. Ta da!

Brian Lands Smoothly in Whistler

Brian hits that drop on the big bike, summer 2004.

In summer 2003, I was riding in Whistler Mountain Bike Park in British Columbia when I took the Clown Shoes trail for the first time. The trail starts with a fun wooden roller coaster, which funnels to a thin log ride through the trees, and then ends in a big diving board that drops six-plus feet to a short slope. I was riding a cross-country bike with clip-in pedals and I'd broken my ankle six weeks before, so a smooth landing was ultra important.

The landing wasn't steep enough or long enough for that drop. I knew if I rolled off it at normal speed I'd go too far and land on flat. On that drop, it was the slower the better. I threaded through the log rides and almost stopped before the drop. It probably looked like I wasn't going to do it.

I cranked my front wheel up, pedaled right off the bridge, and landed without a sound. It felt nice.

Half-Pipe Drop-In

Your buddies are killing the mega half pipe at GnarlSkate2000, the world's raddest skate park. From where you quiver atop the ramp, the coping seems dangerously abrupt and the walls seem impossibly steep. You've never seen anything like this on a trail. If you creep in, you'll catch your rear wheel on the coping. If you fly straight off, you'll land flat bottom—14 feet down. It's time for a drop-in. Uncork this baby on half pipes, quarter pipes, and other types of skate ramps.

1. Ride across the platform, almost parallel to the edge. Get both tires as close to the edge as possible. The closer you get, the less likely your rear tire will clip the coping, and the longer your transition to flat.

2. Turn in and pop your front wheel over the coping. Push your nose down as if you're landing a double, but even more so.

3. Hop your rear wheel over the coping. Make sure you clear the edge. If your rear tire clips, you're looking at a 10-foot flat landing—on your head.

4. Get your tires onto the ramp as soon as possible. Extend your arms and legs. Land with both wheels at the same time or with your front wheel barely first. Ride it out, baby!

Brian's Biggest Drop-In

The old GT building in Huntington Beach, California, had this huge half pipe. It was like 12 feet tall and 20 feet wide, with one or two feet of vert and a short transition. It was built for BMX bikes. It was pretty sketchy, but I came in at an angle and bunny hopped and landed just like it was a steep double. It was actually easier than I thought it would be, but I was still afraid of catching my rear wheel on the lip.

Shoot Your Troubles

Problem: You land hard and bottom your bike. Despite what you might think, this is not cool. Not cool for your bike. Not cool for your body.

Solutions: First of all, make sure you have the right spring rate and sag (see the suspension setup section in chapter 1 on page 12). Then: (1) start the drop with your weight as low on the bike as possible; (2) extend your limbs to get your wheels on the ground as soon as possible; (3) absorb the landing with your arms' and legs' full travel. Important: Don't increase the amplitude until you can land smoothly 1,000 times out of 999 tries.

Problem: On low-speed drops, you land front-wheel first in a gnarly nose wheelie, which quickly leads to head-first landings.

Solutions: Get more pop with your pedals and keep accelerating until both wheels leave the takeoff. Lean back more. Think of doing a really nice manual. If your form is perfect and you're still a nose-heavy nose-lander, try a shorter stem and taller bars. Again, don't mess with drops until you can control the attitude of your bike on flat ground.

Problem: On high-speed drops to downhill landings, you land with the rear wheel first and your front wheel slams hard.

Solution: As always, relax. When you leave the takeoff, match the angle of your bike to the angle of the landing. Your arms will be relatively straight and your legs will be bent. When the front wheel touches down, straighten your legs to contact the ground, then absorb the landing.

Problem: When you drop into a half pipe or something similar, your rear wheel clips the edge.

Solution: First, good luck with your recovery. That 10-foot drop to flat is gonna hurt. Second, as you enter the half pipe, really hop upward and push your front wheel downward. This will help rotate your rear wheel upward.

Whether you ride urban, trails, or full-on freeride, enjoy all kinds of drops. Clunk to flat, sail to downslope, and aim into a vertical wall. When you get the hang of those crazy landings, do you know what comes next? Jumping!

8

Jump With the Greatest of Ease

© Shawn Spomer

You zip along one of your favorite singletracks. A drop falls to your left and a rock outcropping looms ahead. You've always followed the main line around the rocks, but today you're carrying more speed than usual. As you approach the rocks, your mind's eye draws a dotted line straight across them. You're feeling the flow and you let it happen. There's an instant of heavy g's as you pump the face of the first rock, a moment of weightlessness as you fly over the outcropping, and then a gradual re-weighting as you roll down the backside and rail into the turn. Aah . . . if you could bottle that feeling, you'd be rich.

Jumping isn't just for crazy kids. Maybe you want the smoothest way over a rock section. Maybe you'll hit a water bar and find yourself flying, and you want to know what to do. Or maybe you want to have fun on a local slalom course. Whether you're a roadie, a cross-country guy, or a downhill racer, it pays to be at least somewhat comfortable with flight. As they say, "To air is human. To land safely is divine."

Learn to Jump

So you want to learn jumping? Cool. Here's the best way to learn:

1. **Be six years old.**
2. **Go out and play.** Learn by doing. You'll make mistakes and crash, but you're made of rubber and you'll bounce right back up. Learn everything without a hint of self-consciousness or fear.
3. **Keep it up.** Ignore your driver's license, except to drive to cool jumping spots. Lay off the fantasy baseball.
4. **Rip.** There. Easy, right?

We've actually heard guys say, "I'm just gonna hit that lip really fast and see what happens." These goofballs might as well dial 1-800-BROKEN. Assuming you have half a brain, we suggest you start small and learn one step at a time. Never before has learning a dangerous skill been so fun—and easy!

Location, Location, Location

There are two reasons beginners might want to avoid popular jumping spots:

1. The dudes who build jumps care more about huge air and tricks than providing you with a nice, safe jump to learn on. They build stuff big and steep, with gaping holes between takeoff and landing lips. We don't know why, but they always put weird stuff into the gaps: tools, jagged pieces of metal, appliances, that kind of stuff. These guys focus on takeoffs and landings. What's in between means little to them.

Brian's Early Jumps

Lee: Brian, I know this was a long time ago, but do you remember what it was like when you learned how to jump?

Brian: No, but I do remember being five, six, seven years old, pulling stuff out of my garage into the street. We had a bucket and a piece of plywood, and I would just take stuff out of my garage and see what I could jump over.

2. There's usually a bunch of characters hanging around, most of whom are better jumpers than you. If you are self-conscious at all, you'll either feel lame and stay out of their way or you'll feel pressured to try things you're not qualified to do. It's sort of like the adage, "Don't look at supermodels. They will only make you feel fat."

BMX tracks are good places to learn because the jumps are rounded and safe to roll over. It's hard to get a lot of practice, though, with the limited sessions and all the kids asking for your autograph.

Build Your Own

You need a nice beginner's jump.

- ○ **Height:** Two to three feet, with a 1-to-3 height-to-length ratio.
- ○ **Lips:** Yes. Takeoff slightly steeper and more "lippy" than landing.
- ○ **Top:** Flat and about eight feet long to start. You want your entire bike to fit.
- ○ **Approach and run out:** Long, clean, and smooth, with absolutely no rhinos. (They're nothing but trouble.)

This table is perfect for learning. You can land as short as you want without consequence. Of course, Bobbi Kae Watt lands perfectly.

On your "My First Tabletop Jump," you can work on your launching, flying, and landing without worrying about coming up short (smashing into the face of the landing ramp) or impaling yourself on an old shovel handle.

You can start with a single jump and a flat landing, but the ground will be a lot lower than the top of your tabletop, and those landings will hurt. Plus, jumping is all about the feeling you get when you land on the backside. The first time you clear the top of your table, you will be stoked beyond all recognition.

Preflight Checklist

Don't try to be a bloody tough guy. Not "bloody" in the British superlative sense, as in "Steve Peat bloody knows how to party." We mean "bloody" in the vital-fluids-spewing-from-your-body sense.

☐ **Helmet** (preferably full-face)

☐ **Gloves.** Your hands are involved almost every time you crash. When you scrape your palms off, you will miss them.

☐ **Pads.** In order of importance: knee, elbow, hip. Heck, there's nothing wrong with full armor.

☐ **Flat pedals.** Flats allow more foot jive for balance and, of course, they facilitate quick dismounts. If you can't ride in flats, go ahead and run your clip-in pedals. Dork.

☐ **Low seat.** This helps you pump takeoffs and absorb those Evel Knievel landings.

☐ **Reckless disregard.** No, more like a quiet confidence. This should be fun and not at all scary. If you're nervous and tense, save it for another day or find an easier jump.

Jumping basics   A smooth landing comes from a relaxed flight and the perfect takeoff. Sound easy? Keep reading.

Takeoff: Pump the lip just the right amount.

Flight: Stay loose and let the bike move.

Landing: Smooth, baby, smooth.

Takeoff

What you do on the lip determines what happens to you in the air. If you absorb the face of the jump, you stay low. If you press into the face, you go high. If you just sort of ride into the jump, you get bucked over your bars.

Catching good air is all about balance and timing. Here's how to pump a jump to catch moderate air.

1. Coast in a neutral position. Center yourself over the bike, arms and legs slightly bent. Pedals should be level.

2. Crouch down as you approach the jump. Bend your arms and legs to lower your torso.

3. Your crouch should be lowest when you reach the bottom of the face. Note how the front tire is on the face and the rear tire is just reaching it.

4. From your low position, immediately begin to spring upward. Don't hang out in a crouch. Bend down and then immediately pop back up like you're bouncing on a trampoline. This is the crux move.

5. Push down with your arms and legs as you ride up the face. The harder you cram your bike into the face of the jump, the more lift you'll get. Push all the way up the face. Big jumps require a longer, slower push than tiny jumps. For max lift, straighten your arms and legs all the way as you reach the lip.

6. As you leave the lip, bend your arms and legs to let your bike rise into your body. This gives you added clearance, and it helps to keep you loose in the air.

Relax!

If you feel yourself tensing, wiggle your knees and elbows a bit. Gaze over the takeoff toward the landing. Have a "soft" focus. If you're hyper-focused on the lip itself, you'll either stop on it (because you're not ready for what comes next) or you'll be stiff and off balance (because your focus is on the ground, and that's where your body will want to go).

Time Your Jump

When you first get on a diving board or trampoline, you bounce up and down to get a feel for the springiness. You time your jumps so you sink all the way down with maximum down force and spring back up with maximum up force. If you jump up too soon, you get ahead of the upward push, and you don't go very high. If you jump up too late, you get kicked harshly in the feet. It's the same on bike jumps.

   Proper timing depends on a jump's size, your speed, and the springiness of your bike.

	Jump size	Bike speed	Bike suspension
Slow pump	Big	Slow	Soft
Fast pump	Small	Fast	Firm

Flight

In the beginning, just stay over the center of your bike and stay loose, even if you feel off balance. If you relax, your body will balance itself automatically. If you stiffen, you'll stay off balance all the way until you hit the ground.

   When you first start out, it's hard not to be a dead sailor—a stiff and styleless mannequin. To practice proper lack of tension, loosen your grip and move around on your bike. Turn your bars here and there. Do anything but be stiff. Tricks are cool because you have to relax to do them. Eventually, you'll need something to do in the air—mess with your tearoffs or adjust your clutch lever like a motocrosser.

   After you get the hang of this, try bringing your bike up into your body. When you pop off the lip, bend your elbows and knees and let your bike come up toward you. This will help you get extra air and give you more range of motion for pumping the backsides of jumps (see sections on dirt-jumper style and rhythm, pages 106 and 112).

Turning your front wheel in the air helps to stabilize your bike. Stay loose and do whatever feels right.

Landing

To begin with, you should land on the flat top of your tabletop jump.

Land with your back wheel first.   Don't drop the bike. Reach your feet downward, set the rear wheel down, and then bend your knees to absorb the impact. When your front tire lands, use your arms to absorb that impact (see the section on dropping to flat ground, on page 93). You should land like an airplane, only smoother and quieter. But go ahead and make that tire-screeching sound if you want. As you get comfortable, hit your jump with more and more speed.

Spot your landing.   Look where you want to put your wheels, then put them there. This gives you a specific place to aim for and helps your body prepare for a nice landing rather than brace for a random impact. Life lesson: How confident can you be when you have no idea where you're going?

Backside!   Pretty soon your front wheel will start to reach the backside of your landing ramp. The landing will feel much smoother. This is very cool. Be careful not to land with the rear wheel on the end of the flat and your front wheel high in the air. Your front wheel will slam onto the backside really hard, and you might get pitched over the bars.

Try to land with your front wheel first or with both wheels at the same time. While you're in the air, extend your arms to touch the front wheel down on the backside. You're only a touch of speed away from a perfect landing.

Perfect landing.   Your front wheel will land right at the top of the landing ramp, and your rear wheel will land in exactly the same place. When you get it right, you'll hardly have to absorb the impact. The steeper the landing, the smoother

This is a perfect backside landing: Front wheel then rear wheel, in exactly the same place.

How to Land on an Incline

DON'T! But seriously, it's like a super-violent flat landing. Land rear wheel first. Suck it up. Don't be a wimp.

it'll be. After a really steep landing, you can spend the whole day thinking you're still in the air. It's that smooth.

Warning: Jumping is addictive. Small jumps lead to big jumps. Consider yourself warned.

Rigid or Suspension for Jumping?

BMX bikes jump effortlessly. Their tightness returns all the energy you put into the takeoff. Hardtail mountain bikes are more forgiving, but the front suspension and bigger frame and wheels take the edge off the spring action. Suspension bikes are the most forgiving of all, but they suck up a lot of your energy.

PROS OF RIGID

- You can jump higher and faster with less effort.
- You get a better pump in rhythm sections.
- You learn more precise timing.
- Smaller, lighter bikes are easier to whip around in the air.

PROS OF SUSPENSION

- Your timing doesn't have to be as perfect.
- You get a margin of error in case you come up short or land flat.

The bottom line: If you're afraid of hard landings, jump with suspension. If you want to become a great jumper, jump with a hardtail.

Do It Again

When you've been trying to muster the nerve to hit a jump, and you finally do it but maybe not so well, do it again right away. Keep hitting it until you get it dialed—as long as you feel good and aren't making horrible mistakes. When you get it, you'll carry more confidence into your next session.

Dial Your Jumping Style

All jumps are different. They're big, small, tall, short, steep, gradual, on fire, and everything in between. You can hit them with mega speed, or you can botch a turn and arrive too slow. In the real world of dirt jumping, you must alter your style to suit the situation.

The two basic ways to hit a jump are max-air dirt-jumper style and ultra-low racer style. Most jumps require a mix of the two techniques. Learn both and dispense as needed.

Matt Vujicevich pumped this double hard and gets plenty of air in return for his effort.

Curtis Keene sucked up this same jump and stayed nice and low. Same entrance speed, different result.

Get Max Air—Dirt-Jumper Style

This slows you down but gives your bike max loft. Use this technique when you feel like you need to reach for a landing, on really tall, steep dirt jumps where you want to fly high and be a trickster, or on short, lippy jumps where you have to go pretty slow and pump high to catch the backside.

1. Compress your body deep into the lip. It should feel like you're bouncing on a trampoline, trying to get max height.

2. Press against the lip as it pushes your bike upward and backward, creating maximum compression between you and the ground.

3. Explode upward at the very top of the lip. It should feel like a mammoth broad jump.

4. Keep body high and extended on takeoff.

5. Lift the bike up into your body for extra air.

Dirt-jumper style

Mess around. Notice how different timing and oomph affect your height and distance. You'll be amazed at how slow you can go and still clear lips. Compete with your friends to see who can clear a jump the slowest.

Brian Goes Huge at T.J. Lavin's House

T.J. Lavin is a top pro dirt jumper with the coolest backyard in Las Vegas.

I usually like to hit jumps with speed and stay low, but at T.J.'s house he has these 10-foot doubles. They're super steep, and the landings are a foot taller than the takeoffs. I can't suck them up. I have to hit them fast and pump high to make the backsides.

Stay Low—Racer Style

Sometimes you want to keep your momentum, barely clear the landing, and then get back to business. This isn't just a racing technique: Use it when you're going so fast you might overshoot a jump. Here's how to suck up a jump at speed.

1. Let your bike roll into the lip but keep your body high. If there's a small dip before the lip, keep your body high and push your bike into the hole.

2. Coast up the lip without pressing down. With dirt-jumper style, you want max tension between your bike and the face of the jump. In racer style, you want as little tension as possible.

3. "Suck up" the lip. As you reach the top and the lip pushes your bike upward and backward, bend your arms and legs and let the bike move back into your body. It's the opposite of the dirt-jumper explosion. It's more like an implosion. Don't force any energy into the ground; absorb it all with your body.

4. Keep your body low and compressed on takeoff.

5. Push the bike forward a bit to get you over the center.

Racer style

Light in transition. — Absorb lip. — Body low, bike held close. — Suck up to clear landing lip. — "Must ... go ... faster."

You maintain speed.

26 mph — 25 mph

Play around with this. See how fast you can go without overshooting the landing.

Save Yourself

You might be going too slow, or maybe you didn't pump hard enough. Either way, you're coming up short. There are some things you can do.

Lower your landing gear. If you're not going to make the landing, you'll know it as soon as you take off. This is the one situation where picking your nose is a bad thing. Lift the front end, drop the rear, and brace for impact.

Pick up your bike. If you feel like you're not going quite fast enough to clear the jump, use your best dirt-jumper style and pump the heck out of the face. As you leave the lip, pull your bike up with your arms and legs.

Double pump it. You're flying along and it's clear you won't quite make the landing. This all happens in the fraction of a second.

- ○ Lift your bike just a bit.
- ○ Push it down.
- ○ Violently pull it back up. The up-and-down dynamic gives you more upward mojo than a single lift.

Lift your rear wheel.   Say your front wheel is going to clear the backside but you need a little something extra to get your rear wheel over the lip.

- ○ Grip the bars really tightly.
- ○ Rotate your hands forward as you push forward and down.
- ○ Lift your feet as the rear end comes up.

Abandon ship.   If things look messy, let go and try to land on your feet. Tuck and roll. Keep your arms and legs inside until the ride comes to a complete stop.

Brian Goes HUGE

How far you can jump a bike has yet to be determined. With the right jump, the right speed, and the right landing, there's no reason you can't go over 100 feet. That kind of jumping isn't normal, so most people aren't comfortable with it.

When I did that huge jump for *ChainSmoke 2*, it was a little scary the first time. The actual jump wasn't that tall—the takeoff was three feet, then it dropped five feet and there was a long tabletop with a long landing. The thing was, I was going so fast. I knew I wouldn't get hurt if I came up short, but I knew it would be harsh. When I hit it the first time, it popped me higher than I expected and I flew 87 feet. The next few times I didn't go as fast, and I went only 75 or 80 feet to backside. It was actually pretty easy once I got used to the speed.

The time I broke my thumb at Bubba Stewart's moto track in 2003, I wasn't scared at all. The double was 53 feet, with an 8- to 10-foot takeoff and landing. I couldn't get enough speed on my bike, so I got pulled in with a quad. I was too nonchalant about it. I had no experience getting pulled by a moto, but I was never worried. I was in the air a long time. When I realized I was coming up short, I brought my front wheel as high as I could. I thought, "Uh-oh, this is going to be hard." I was worried about breaking my ankles, which were already hurt. But I landed and my ankles were fine; I broke my thumb instead.

Handle All Sorts of Jumps

After you master different lips, jumping styles, distances, and landings, you're ready to step up to the fun stuff. These advanced jumps require solid all-around skills, so if you haven't done your homework, expect to be grounded.

Sail Over Doubles

Doubles are a total mind trip. Technically, they're identical to tabletops. You pop off the takeoff ramp, you fly through the air, and then you land on the backside. The fact there's a gaping hole between the lips should make no difference to you. But it does. Right now in the world, 1,389 riders are intimidated by doubles that would be pieces of cake if the gaps were filled with nice, smooth dirt. This is a classic case of being afraid of what *might* happen.

Brian gets a little practice session in his backyard. When you're confident like this, a double is no harder than a comparable table.

When you jump in the real world, you usually jump over something: a rock, a stream, a big hole with a shovel in it. You should learn to judge takeoffs and land-ings so you don't have to worry about landing in random, terrible places. Don't tackle a double until you can perfectly backside a tabletop of the same persua-sion. You should not hurl your carcass off a lip unless you believe you'll actually reach the landing. Start small and slowly work your way up.

If the takeoff and landing are at the same elevation, jumping a double is exactly like jumping a tabletop with the same shape. That said, here are some things to keep in mind:

- **Spot your landing** and then scan forward from there. Do not look into the hole. Stop it!

- **Get your back tire over the lip,** especially when the front of the landing ramp is sharp and steep. Conundrum: If you prepare yourself for clipping the lip, you'll drop your feet and you *will* hit the lip.

- **Nail step-downs:** When the landing lies below the takeoff, you don't need as much speed or pump to land cleanly. You have extra vertical speed by the time you fall to the landing, so coming up short hurts more than usual.

You maintain speed over step-downs. Note the backside boost on landing.

Brian's Favorite Step-Up

While I was in Japan visiting a GT distributor, we drove out to these dirt jumps. The traffic was terrible, but when we finally got there, there was this huge area with jumps, all sweet and perfect. They were some of the nicest jumps I've ever done. The coolest thing was, you came into this berm, and as it went downhill, it turned over 360 degrees, like a corkscrew. At the bottom, you hit this step-up and jumped back over the berm. It was the raddest thing ever.

○ **Step up to step-ups:** When the landing towers above the takeoff, you need extra speed and pump to clear it. Rhythm sections contain step-ups because they give you extra-jumbo backside. Step-ups are visually arresting—all you see is a wall of dirt—but the landings are actually smoother than step-downs and normal doubles. If you hit a step-up just right, you can set your bike softly on the landing, like a mother bird landing in her nest. How nice.

Carry extra speed into step-ups because the vert lip will slow you down.

Why Aren't All Jumps Tabletops?

Moving dirt is a lot of work. Why would an expert jumper fill in a gap he will never enter?

Longevity. Lips wear down when people roll over them. Nobody wants to roll into the chasm of death, so scary doubles last longer than tables.

Pump Rhythms

If there's one thing you should learn on your bike, it's jumping rhythm. When you get it right, it feels perfectly smooth, and the rhythmic weight-then-weightlessness is one of the most exquisite feelings on earth.

Curtis Keene enters a sweet set at The Shells in Redwood City, California.

A rhythm section is usually a series of closely spaced double jumps. As you come down one landing, you transition immediately into the next takeoff. You must rhythmically pump the transitions to create speed for the jumps. Rhythm is a puzzle. You must get the first piece in order to get the second. If you screw up one double, the next is very hard to make.

Warning: Don't mess with rhythm until you've mastered double jumps. You should be able to handle a variety of lips, steepnesses, and speeds. Things go wrong quickly in rhythm.

TIPS FOR SIMPLE RHYTHM

○ **Land as high as possible** on the landing ramp, front wheel first, followed by your rear wheel on the same spot. Do this with German precision.

○ **Press down** into your pedals as you reach the bottom of the face. You will feel an amazing acceleration. On a steep landing, it feels like the gas is wide open.

○ **Stay sharp.** Adjust for varying distance, steepness, and speed. The most interesting rhythms require all of your jumping kung fu. Let's see what you've got.

Pumping rhythm   After you land the first jump, a good pump will more than double your speed for the second one.

—10 mph—   ———23 mph———   —9 mph—

Combine Rollers and Jumps

When you approach a set of rollers—or any takeoff and potential landing—consider the depth of the gap, the lippiness of the takeoff, and your speed. The deeper the gap, the more you want to jump clear of the downside. In order to jump, you need a certain amount of lip. If the lip is steep, you can hit it pretty slowly and pump it dirt-jumper style. If the lip is gradual, you need lots of speed. If you don't have enough speed to clear the gap, go ahead and manual across—and pump the backside for free speed while you're at it.

TO SUM IT UP

Deep gap + steep lip + fast approach = jump

Shallow gap + gradual lip + slow approach = roll or manual

Safety Crank

Sometimes you need more speed to clear a lip. Maybe you blew a backside. Maybe the next jump is huge or far away. If you're in the right gear and a fast-twitch fiend, you can sneak in half a crank. This is a good reason to practice jumping with your opposite foot forward.

Rhythm sections on BMX and bikercross tracks include various combinations of obstacles: single rollers, multiple rollers, tables, step-ups, step-downs, and maybe some banana splits. These rhythms are ultra fun. They allow myriad approaches, from simply rolling all the way through to combining jumps and manuals in a stunning display of biking prowess.

BMX rhythm   This section at Dacono BMX in Dacono, Colo., looks simple but gives you plenty to play with.

Jump Hips

The only thing cooler than jumping is turning while you jump. You can't actually arc sideways while you're in the air, but you can rotate your bike so you land facing a new direction. Do this when a jump sits in a turn.

1. Look where you want to go and turn your bike across the lip of the jump.
2. Throw your head and body into the turn.
3. Turn your bars the way you want to go, and let the rear end swing around to the angle you want.
4. Straighten your bars to match the landing and suck it up, baby!

Get a Transfer

In a transfer jump, you jump to the side but land in basically the same direction you took off. You can use this to jump from line to line on a trail, or to jump from one line of jumps to another.

1. Ride across the lip in the direction you want to go. As always, look ahead.

2. Fly straight toward your target. Whee!

3. As you approach your landing, push down on your inside grip and turn your bars outward. This and a little body English will whip your rear end around and lean your bike a bit. You're setting yourself up to make a little turn down the backside of the jump.

4. Right before touchdown, turn your bars into the landing. This will straighten your bike and set you up for the next thing. Sweet.

Know Your Packs

The cool people refer to rhythm sections as "six-packs" or "ten-packs" or whatever-number packs. A six-pack is three doubles, for a total of three lips and three landings.

Jump Into Turns

For the ultimate in three-dimensional fun, hit a double and land in a berm. It's easier than it seems: Handle the corner as if there's no jump and handle the jump as if there's no corner.

1. Set up for the turn as you leave the jump.
2. Fly toward the outside of the corner. You might need your hip or transfer skills.
3. Land with your wheels perpendicular to the ground. If you land in a left-hand berm, pitch your wheels out to the right, as if you're already railing the corner. You *will* be railing it in a second.
4. You're dropping into the berm with a lot of force, so you might as well pump it for some extra exit speed (see section on pumping berms, page 70).

Lay Your Bike Flat

Few things are as stylish as laying your bike over in a nice, flat tabletop. In addition, tables let you pitch your bike over to land in a turn. Here's how to lay your bike down to the left:

Do a tabletop to the left   Do the opposite to lay your bike to the right.

1. Takeoff is pretty normal.

2. Turn your bars to the left.

3. Push your bike downward with your left hand and knee.

4. Keep pushing down with your left hand, letting the bike pivot around its mid point. Style for the camera.

5. To prepare for landing, straighten your bars and uncoil your legs.

6. Land just like normal—nice and smooth!

TABLE TIPS

○ Hip jumps make it easy to flatten your bike, since you're already slipping sideways through the air. It's hard to get your bike out, flat, and back again while you're going straight.

○ You can get your bike flatter when your front foot is on the bottom side. If you jump with your right foot forward, you'll rule at laying your bike to the right. You'll suck at doing it to the left. Sorry.

Turn Down

If a tabletop is a stylish dirt jumper, the turn down is his racer brother. A turn down keeps your body low and gets your front wheel on the ground early. It works best when you're hipping or transferring, and you're going so fast you'll overclear the jump. To see an ultra-high-speed turn down in action, watch James "Bubba" Stewart on a motocross track.

Turn it down   Uncork this baby next time you jump through a turn with way too much speed.

1. Lean and turn across the face of the jump.

2. Turn your front wheel down.

3. Push your bike down.

4. Straighten your bars for landing.

5. Land front wheel first.

Say you want to turn down into a left:

1. Turn across the face of the jump. This gets your body lower than if you ride straight off.

2. When your front wheel takes off, turn it even farther to the left, down toward the ground. Ha! See? A "turn down."

3. Push your bike down. Keep turning the bars and let the rear end whip around.

4. Straighten your bars. Turn the wheel the direction you want to go, then begin to straighten your arms and legs. At this speed it's easy to overclear the downslope, so really push your bike down to catch backside.

5. Land front wheel first. The rear end might be whipped around when it lands, but that's okay. As long as you're steering in the direction you're heading, it's all good.

Bump Jump

You can use a square rock or curb as a takeoff to jump over a section. The challenge is, if you bash your front wheel into such an abrupt edge, it'll slow you down or knock you silly. In a bump jump you clear your front wheel and literally bump your rear wheel into the object, letting it bounce you skyward. Compared with bashing front-wheel first, a bump jump preserves momentum and maintains control. Before you try this move, make sure you have manuals and jumps dialed.

Bump jump   Here's a nifty trick for those of you who have wired manuals and jumps.

1. Manual as you approach your takeoff.

2. Bump the rock with your back wheel.

3. Enjoy your flight. Stay back if you want to keep your nose up.

Keep Pedaling Over a Jump

The gate drops and you explode with pedal-spinning fury. You and three other hungry racers, that is. A tabletop jump or roller lies between you and the first turn. This is no time to sail through the air—you gotta keep the power on.

1. As you approach the hump, manual to get your front wheel up. You don't want your wheel bonking the face of the jump.

2. As your bike rides up the face, suck the bike up into you. Get way low and way back.

3. If it's a short hump, as in this photo, stay back on the bike and keep pedaling. If it's a long table, get over the center of your bike and pedal like normal, but as you reach the end of the table, get back over the rear of your bike.

4. When you reach the downslope, pull on the bars and push the rear of your bike down. This will give you lots of power, plus some nice backside. Keep pedaling!

To pedal over a series of humps, repeat this move: high, low, high, low. Braap braaap!

Shoot Your Troubles

Problem: You land way short.

Solutions: Either go faster or pump the takeoff harder. If you're already riding fast, sucking up the lip and staying low will take you farther than if you pop into the air.

Problem: You get off balance in the air.

Solution: Relax! Stay loose and make corrections in the air. If you can't hit a jump in a relaxed state, you have no business hitting that jump. A stiff takeoff might send you funny, and a stiff flight will likely result in a messy landing.

Problem: Your front wheel finds perfect backside, but your rear wheel clips the landing. You still roll down the ramp, but you lose a lot of speed.

Solution: Chances are your legs are too straight and your rear wheel is too low. Have someone watch you. If your front wheel and body are flying like the riders who are making it, then this is an issue of overzealous landing gear. When most of us get nervous, we tend to extend our legs in preparation for a hard landing. You must believe you'll make it. As you take off, let your bike and feet float up into your body. Don't extend your legs until your landing is underfoot, if you know what we're saying.

Problem: You land hard.

Solutions: Try to land on downslopes. Land with soft, extended arms and legs and try to use your full body-suspension travel.

Problem: You can handle tabletops no problem, but doubles scare the heck out of you.

Solutions: Become hyperconfident on tables of the same ilk before you go for the double action. Second, stop staring into the gap. Instead, look softly somewhere beyond the landing.

Problem: You strain to generate speed in rhythm, you have a hard time moving your bike in the air, or you feel a bit out of control.

Solutions: You probably have too much upper-body tension. This is huge! Totally relax your upper body. Stand on your pedals and let your hands float on the grips. Play a game with your friends: Watch each other, and if you see any muscular tension in the air or in the transitions, you have to do 10 push-ups. (Unfortunately, the push-ups might make you even tighter.) If you can relax your upper body, you will immediately notice better flow, more pump, and a whole new level of style in your jumping. Like we said, THIS IS HUGE!

Jumping is the ultimate expression of bike mastery. It's no coincidence that every great jumper is also an exceptional trail rider. (The opposite can't be said for trail riders.) Jumping is fun and addictive on its own, but it also helps you flow better in every situation.

Flow on Any Trail

W hen you learn to brake, pedal, corner, hop, drop, and jump, you can get yourself over, around, or through just about any obstacle. That's a fine start. But to flow down a trail—to experience the ultimate joy of mountain biking—takes more.

See Better to Go Faster

If you want to smash into a rock, do this: Zip along a trail. See a rock. Stare at the rock. As you get closer, slow down and lower your head to keep the rock locked in your gaze. Since your bike points at the rock, chances are you'll smash into it. When you stare at a rock, you tell your brain, "Rock. Rock. Rock!" Your brain does the only thing it can with that information: It gives you a rock.

In order to guide you down a smooth line, your brain needs better info to work with.

See as fast as you ride. You can only ride as fast as you can scan the trail. When your eyes slow down and look closer to your front wheel, you have to slow down. When your eyes speed up and scan farther ahead, you can speed up. Keep scanning ahead; never lock your eyes on anything.

Raise your gaze. When you drive a car on a dark country road, your high beams let you see farther and drive faster. Think of your eyes as high beams: point them as far down the trail as you can. When you swoop through a redwood forest at 10 mph, follow the light soil 20 feet ahead of you. When you haul down the Kamikaze downhill, look for the white gravel 100 yards ahead. If you look farther down the trail, you will immediately become a better rider. Know why?

When you elevate your gaze, you literally elevate your perception of the trail. Instead of noticing individual objects—little round rock, big pointy rock, huge wet rock—you sense the overall flow of the trail—left, right, up, and down. A rock waterfall scares most riders at Northstar at Tahoe mountain bike park in California. Hundreds of head-sized and bigger rocks jumble down a steep slope. A lumpy chicane crosses halfway down. At the bottom, a four-foot slab drops into a flat, dusty turn. Most riders clatter down one rock at a time— bap, bap, bap, bap, bap—barely make the left, flounder through the right, creep down the drop, and then blow the turn. The fastest pros see the section at a higher level: a descent, a transfer, and then the drop. They pump the first pitch, whip their bikes over the chicane, float off the drop, and rail the corner. They project their attention beyond the rocks toward their ultimate goal—that final corner.

The higher you look, the lower your perceived speed—and the faster you can ride. Next time you drive down the freeway, look straight out your side window and try to count the dashed lines in your lane. They whiz by too fast, don't they? Look a hundred yards ahead and notice how the dashes seem to slow down. By looking

Lee Hops Over a Dead Fan

While I was at Humboldt State University, Jerry Garcia of the Grateful Dead got sick, and hundreds of aimless Dead fans took over the town where I lived. The locals soon chased the drifters away, and most of them camped in the community forest. One morning while I railed my favorite singletrack, I came around a turn and— whoa!—people were sleeping all over the place. One dude was right in front of me, and I hopped right over him. Good thing I was paying attention.

ahead, you give yourself more time to deal with situations: a tight turn, a rock, a Dead fan sleeping in your path.

You're a flashlight, not a laser.   Sweep your eyes over an area a few feet wide that encompasses your line and the obstacles or landmarks around it. Say you're cruising down the National Trail in Phoenix, Arizona. You don't want to be thinking, "Rock right, cactus left. Rock, cactus, drop. . . ." Instead, see the ribbon of smooth dirt, and just kind of *feel* the boundaries.

Beware the magnetic rock.   When you see something scary—a rock, a gap in a double jump, whatever—notice it but keep your eyes moving. As you approach the object of your fixation, you unconsciously aim for it, slow down to keep it in view, and fail to plan for the next situation. How many times have you bashed right into that rock you were trying to avoid? How many times have you cleared a rocky climb and then fallen on a smooth section? When you fill your focus with one thing, there's no space to deal with anything else.

Your Eye: The Right Tool for the Job

Your most detailed vision concentrates in the center of where you're looking, in a cone about 15 degrees wide. If you're looking 25 feet down a trail, your area of highest focus is about 6 feet wide. As you approach the side of your vision, the level of detail goes down, but your ability to track movement goes up. So what does this mean? Use your high-definition vision to choose lines as far ahead as possible. As you approach obstacles, let your peripheral vision do what it does best: keep track of the obstacles and tell your brain when it's time to hop, skip, or jump.

Focus on what's important—the sweet line straight over the rock—and let your peripheral vision handle everything else.

Under your wheels, out of your mind. The root crossing the trail isn't going anywhere. Keep scanning ahead and trust your automatic ability to get over it. When you walk up a set of stairs, do you stare at every single step? Of course not. If you do, maybe mountain biking isn't for you. Shoot, maybe *walking* isn't for you.

Connect the dots. When you read a trail, you design a giant connect-the-dots puzzle. If you stare at individual scary things, your puzzle will have only a few dots, and your path will be herky jerky. The faster and more fluidly you can process many points, the smoother your line will be.

Look at the things that matter. Note your turning points and watch out for obstacles you have to ride around. Ignore everything else. Experienced riders know what they need to pay attention to: boulders, cliffs, and trees. Novices waste effort looking at things that don't matter: gravel, tiny ruts, and small woodland creatures.

Pick Great Lines

A trail is a blank canvas: an area framed by rocks, foliage, course tape, or thousand-foot cliffs in which you render your mountain bike masterpiece. Since your tires only need a path a few inches wide, your choices are nearly endless. This is the most complicated aspect of mountain biking. You have to balance speed, terrain, equipment, skills, risk, and your goals—all while your heart pounds and your eyeballs rattle out of your head. So where do you start?

The normal line is left around the rotten log. The fast line is straight over the log.

If you're just cruising, especially for the first time on that trail, go ahead and follow the worn line. The path most traveled weaves around obstacles and provides the smoothest, easiest route from point A to point B. A thousand happy mountain bikers can't all be wrong, can they?

Well, yes, they can. A line that avoids every little obstacle has lots of curves, many of them quite tight. Most riders dive into corners too early, creating slow exit lines. For low speeds and climbing, the smooth line works just fine. But as your speed increases, you have a harder time making all the corners. You can't flip your bike around each and every rock, and your cornering g's overpower the available traction. You could slow down, but that's no fun. Instead, look for straighter lines and smoother arcs. Flow right over the rocks instead of slaloming around them. Line up wide for corners, carve all the way inside, and exit wide, even where roots crisscross the trail. Experiment to figure out what you can ride over without losing speed or killing yourself. As you zoom down a trail, avoid these "threshold" obstacles. Otherwise, go straight down the straights and carve mathematically perfect arcs around the corners. As world champion downhiller Steve Peat says, "Use the whole trail. Don't be a sheep."

The Tunnel Trail in Santa Barbara, California, consists of slabs of jumbled, weirdly eroded sandstone. There's no obvious "easy" line—just rock, rock, and more rock. You have to let your eyes scan quickly for the smoothest routes: water gullies, worn-down rock, or scrubbed-off tire tread. Make your best choice, but be ready in case you encounter something gruesome. An average Joe can creep over a foot-high, round stone. A pro downhiller can bound over a four-foot boulder. As your skills and confidence increase, you'll find yourself sailing and railing over things that now terrify you, flowing straight down the trail like water.

Turning Is Turning

I (Lee) was asking my friend Curtis Keene, one of the United States' fastest pro downhillers, which line he would take if a big bump sat in the middle of a turn.

"Well," Curtis said, "if the bump wasn't in a turn, how would you ride over it?"

I told him I'd suck up the frontside and pump the backside.

"OK, what line would you take if the turn didn't have a hump in it?"

I told him I'd line up wide, sweep inside, then exit wide.

"Well, there you go."

Ah hah! Turning is turning, and getting over stuff is getting over stuff. If a turn has weird stuff in it, it's still a turn, and the best line is still the best line, except you're riding over stuff while you're at it.

Of course, this approach requires that you can get over whatever's in the turn without any hassle. Little rocks and ruts are okay. Boulders and alligators, you might have to ride around.

A Line for Every Purpose

Cruising: On any well-used trail, a worn path meanders among the obstacles and cuts easy if not perfect arcs through the corners. This is literally "the path most traveled." It's usually the safest way down the trail. Perfect for leisure, exploration, and learning.

Racing: Whether cross-country or downhill, you want the fastest, straightest lines your current skills, equipment, and conditions can handle.

Freeriding: This is all about fun. Time is no worry, and it seems like safety isn't much of a worry, either. Depending on your level, you might veer off the main line to drop off a stump, or you might huck off a 40-foot cliff. There seem to be no limits, and the regular rules of speed and efficiency do not apply.

Dial In Your Speed

The IMBA would like us to say we love mountain biking because it helps us appreciate nature. But when you ask riders what they love most about our fine sport, most say "speed." Whether on foot, skis, surfboard, camel, car, or jet, we humans have an innate need to haul ass.

Fast is definitely more fun than slow, but the real measure of pleasure is perceived speed: the sensations of sight, sound, and movement. Ten mph on a bike with gravel crunching and trees whooshing past is a lot more stimulating than 650 mph in an airliner with cellophane crinkling and the snack cart squeaking by. Beginners love the howling wind, the skittering tires, and the very notion they're riding a bike so fast on dirt. Experts tend to focus on the feelings of acceleration and deceleration, swooping in and out of turns, and flying over obstacles. It's the same level of excitement, with a different focus.

Every line has a range of viable speeds. Flat, easy lines have a wide range; it doesn't matter whether you go fast or slow. Steep, gnarly lines have a narrow range of speed—too slow and you can't carry over rough stuff; too fast and you lose control. As a matter of fact, the gnarlier the line is, the more speed you need and the more you must commit. Speed helps you float over the tops of rocks, hop farther over roots, whip through corners, and carry momentum through violent sections. When the going gets really steep and silly, braking screws up your bike's handling, and you can't really slow down anyway. You just have to surrender yourself to the hill.

Speed is like voltage. It pushes you down the trail, through corners, and over rises. It stimulates your senses and gives you a thrill. Of course, the higher the voltage, the stronger the shock. In general, the optimum speed lets you get over obstacles, make corners, react to surprises, and have fun. People who try to haul

In a rock garden like this you want to go fast enough to carry over the rocks but slow enough to stay in control. Zach Griffith strikes a nice balance.

ass before they master the basics crash often and hard. That's a dangerous, counterproductive way to become a fast rider. Instead, concentrate on being smooth. Speed will come.

Ride With a Reserve

It's a crazy, random world out there.

Say you're out riding 100 percent. You're right on the edge of control, and I'll bet you're having fun. But if something happens—a flat tire, an unexpected rock, a surprise hiker—you have nowhere to go but down.

If, on the other hand, you ride at 80 percent, you still have a 20 percent reserve of traction and mental acuity to deal with the inevitable. You should always ride with some reserve. The right amount depends on the situation.

0 to 10 percent reserve. Timed race run. You want to win, but is a ruptured spleen worth a plastic medal?

25 percent reserve. Weekend ride in a public park. Two words: Sierra Club.

50 percent reserve. Expedition in the middle of nowhere. Two words: Wolf food.

75 percent reserve. Riding a dirt road with your arm in a sling, which one of the authors (Lee) admits to having done. Two words: Dumb ass.

Commit

Whatever you do, you must do it with confidence. On terrain that you find easy, you can cruise along pretty much however you like: fast, slow, standing on the saddle, or whatever. When the situation only calls for half your abilities, you can get away using half your wits. But the more a situation tests your skills and confidence, the more committed you have to be. There's a nice paradox here; when you're most nervous, that's when you have to find it within yourself to commit 100 percent. Crazy.

Failure to commit leads to failure to stay on your bike. If you try to corner without leaning, you follow a tangent into the poison oak. If you try to jump too slowly, you land on top of the school bus. If you try to hop a curb without really snapping upward, you ruin your rear wheel, and the cheerleaders laugh at you.

When the line is smooth, you can roll along a nice, easy two-dimensional line around the mushrooms, past the fairy princess' chalet and up to the gingerbread

See It to Be It

Don't step up the magnitude until your current riding is smooth and consistent, and you can visualize yourself succeeding in the new move. If you can't envision yourself riding a technical section perfectly, don't even try. If you approach with a squiggle above your head, you will fail. Here's an example from Lee:

At the 2003 Big Bear national downhill, a big step-down at the bottom of the expert course scared me to death. People were getting hurt like crazy. I knew I could handle it, but I just didn't know how it would feel. As I walked up to session the jump, a guy crashed right in front of me. He broke his arm and ankle, and he cried for morphine the entire time I held him, which was almost 40 minutes. That was hard. After a dozen false starts, I finally hit the jump a few times—perfectly, I might add. The morning of the race, a Japanese pro woman died on that jump, and I found out a friend paralyzed himself the day before. As I spun the trainer at the start house, I could see myself riding every bit of the course perfectly—except that jump. When I thought of it, I felt heavy fear and saw nothing but blackness. I raced the course fine, but as I approached the jump my mind went blank. I half-committed, cased on my front wheel, and cartwheeled into the crowd. In that state of mind, I should have taken the bailout.

house. The rougher the line, the more three-dimensional your path becomes. You have to hop over moats, manual over smoldering villages, and dive into tight turns. This rapid weighting and unweighting requires you to scan critically for your line and commit 100 percent to throwing your bike around.

Low-Commitment, Low-Risk Riding

Low-commitment riding, aka "cruising," is slow and mellow. Mud might make you nervous. A mellow trail might bore you. Or you might be 50 miles from a rest at Everest base camp, and a crash might mean certain death.

- Pick the smoothest, easiest lines even if you have to ride around obstacles.
- Keep your speed down.
- Pedal softly and efficiently.

Brian on Rebuilding Confidence

In spring of 2004, I broke my ankle and I was off the bike for two and a half months. When the bone healed, I started riding XC, and I felt good on regular trails. I didn't feel like I lost much, but when I got on the slalom bike and started sprinting and jumping, that's when I started to feel rusty. I didn't want to crash, and I just didn't feel confident—like, "How will my leg feel if I hit that lip really hard?"

When you get to a certain level, you always keep 75 percent of your skills. You can go out and ride any time at that level. But it's that last part that separates the good guys from the great guys. At a downhill race where most pros run 7:00 and the winners run 6:00 or 6:10, the winners could run 6:20s all day long. Those guys have total confidence to go that speed, and their race runs are no big deal to them.

Time is the main thing. I have to have my leg feel good so I can go into situations with total confidence; that way, if I push hard and something happens, I won't get hurt. I know how to do these things; I just have to get comfortable doing them.

Regaining confidence after an injury is a lot like building confidence as you step up your riding. You're not going to go from jumping a 5-foot double straight to a 25-foot double. You have to be smart about it, or the whole process will take a lot longer. When you try something, you have to have the confidence to know you can do it. That comes from experience and knowledge, and time spent on the bike. Over the years, you learn how to react to different jumps, speeds, lips, distances, and so on.

On motos, if we both have 250s, I can tell you to hit a jump in third gear half open, but everyone has different bike strength, so I can't tell you how hard to pedal. You just have to start gradually and build up your experience and confidence to go bigger.

- Brake lightly to slow down gradually.
- Steer gently.
- Let your bike roll slowly over rough terrain.

High-Commitment Riding

High-commitment riding, aka "ripping," is fast and aggressive. You might be hauling the mail on a familiar trail. Loose dirt might force you to commit to a steep pitch. Or you might be railing the Vermont national downhill course, and a win would mean free tires for life. (Whoo yeah, I'd risk almost anything for that!)

- Pick the straightest lines, even if they go over gnarly stuff.
- Go fast.
- Pedal aggressively.
- Brake hard to slow down quickly.
- Lean and press hard into corners.
- Manual, hop, or jump over everything in your path.

Choose Your Pill

You're zooming down National Downhill at Whistler Mountain Bike Park, British Columbia. The trail is steep, tight, and rough, but at least it's made of dirt. You cross a dirt road and drop into Clown Shoes. Before you know it, you're riding a wooden roller coaster—whoa!—which soon funnels to a foot-wide, five-foot-high log ride. Yikes! You feel like Neo in *The Matrix*. What do you do?

Take the blue pill. *The story ends. You wake in your bed and believe whatever you want to believe.* Stop and walk around the section. You won't gain anything, but you won't lose anything, either. The thing is, how content can you be once you know what's out there?

Take the red pill. *Stay in Wonderland and see how deep the rabbit hole goes.* Sometimes you just have to take the red pill. Dive into the unknown. Have faith in your skills and experience. More often than not, your commitment will carry you through. Your world will never be the same.

Pump Terrain for Free Speed

"Astounding Breakthrough Promises More Speed With Less Pedaling!"

"Ride Uphill Without Turning Your Legs!"

"Monkey-Boy Seen Riding Pedal-Less Bike!"

If you throw in a set of steak knives, mountain bikers would line up for this miracle. The truth is, behind this hype lies a very cool and simple fact: When you push down on a short downslope, you get a forward boost. This is called "pumping."

Pedaling can't be beaten for pure efficiency, but pumping lets you accelerate where you can't pedal: when obstacles are too close to each other, the ground is too rough, or you've leaned too far. There's no room to pedal between doubles in a rhythm section. Pedals get smashed in rock gardens. And pedals strike the ground in corners. A good pump lets you gain speed in these situations.

Pumping terrain 101   When you master pump, your riding will improve in ways you can't imagine. Let's start with a basic BMX roller.

1. Load your bike as you approach the roller.   **2.** Suck it up and lean forward.   **3.** Push down the backside: arms first, then legs.

TO PUMP UP YOUR RIDING:

Look for your opportunities.   Actively seek pumpworthy lines. The fronts of holes and the backs of humps, rocks, logs, and roots all beg to be pumped. Great riders seldom coast along; they constantly wring speed from the terrain.

Unload the fronts.   Beware frontsides. At best they slow you down. At worst they buck you into oblivion. Before you pump the back, you have to get over the front. You can unload, manual, hop, jump, or skip. Do whatever suits your fancy, as long as you have enough range of motion to push down the back—and as long as you don't bash into the thing full force.

Pump a manual.   When the bumps are so close together that your front wheel climbs one while your rear wheel drops another, manual your front tire out of the way and pump that rear tire. To see this in action, watch BMX and bikercrossers motor through huge rhythm sections.

Pump small things.   You don't need a long ramp. Pump happens at the transition between vertical and flat. All you need is a little slope, a rock, or even a tiny root. Anything is better than nothing.

Pump rough things.   If you try to pedal through a jumbly rock garden, you'll stab a pedal and catapult onto your noggin. If you try to coast, you'll bog down and fall on your shoulder. We say bah-hooey to both of those options. Instead, try to pump the backsides of the bigger rocks. A rock garden threatens a hundred ways to kill you, but it promises a hundred places to catch backside.

Pump on uphills.   You can use the pump on any downslope, even if it's on a climb. Say an uphill trail dips into a creek bed and then climbs the opposite bank. Pedal your arse off as usual, then pump the slope down into the bed. Unload as you zoom up the rise, and you'll be golden.

Pump berms.   A berm is just a sideways hole. Try loading the entrance and unloading the exit.

Pump under load.   You can hit a berm or dip with so much force it's hard to pedal. What to do? Pump, of course!

Remember: A nice backside will take you far—in life and in bike riding.

Brian's Most Pumpworthy Trail

The Whoops Trail in Santa Monica isn't very steep, but in a few miles it has like 150 rollers. It seems like someone left piles of dirt on the trails, and they just sort of wore the way they are. Kids built lips to the sides of some of 'em, but for the most part they're pretty random. It takes a few runs in a row to remember what's coming. You can roll over the small rollers and manual the round ones, and as you pump 'em you get going really fast. Some of the rollers are really lippy with no backsides, so you have to jump. It's tricky, though, because on some you land flat, or you bonk your front wheel and lose speed.

Find a State of Flow

Mountain biking satisfies so many desires. It transforms a gunnysack full of kittens into a ripped, hard body. It carries you through stunning places with exceptional people. Its sites, sounds, smells, and sensations block out all your inner demons. And, of course, the speed and magnitude of it all excite you like nothing else.

You can go for half a dozen rides and enjoy them for half a dozen reasons. Your lunchtime loop keeps you fit, Moab's Porcupine Rim Trail enthralls you, a twisty singletrack whips you like a roller coaster, a huge jump scares the heck out of you.

These are all fantastic ways to enjoy our fine sport, but the ultimate experience happens when your thoughts crawl into your CamelBak and your body flows along the trail without effort or voice. Time changes. Tension disappears. You're focused but not forced. Controlling your bike becomes effortless. You've entered the magical state of "flow."

Dr. Mihaly Csikszentmihalyi describes the feeling of flow in his groundbreaking book, *Flow: The Psychology of Optimal Experience:* ". . . Concentration is so intense that there is no attention left over to think about anything irrelevant, or to worry about problems. Self-consciousness disappears, and the sense of time becomes distorted. An activity that produces such experiences is so gratifying that people are willing to do it for its own sake, with little concern for what they will get out of it, even when it is difficult, or dangerous."

Does that sound familiar?

Flow only happens when the demands of the situation intersect with your abilities. The trail isn't so hard it scares you, nor is it so easy it bores you. The further the demands lay above your perceived abilities, the bigger the rush. Savor a peaceful cruise down a local trail, enjoy a thrill behind a faster rider down a new path, or transcend all you thought possible by pinning it for an entire cross-country race. You might vomit at the end, but it feels so good, doesn't it?

We say "perceived" abilities because that's what counts. Most of us can climb harder, corner faster, and fly farther than we usually do. When you can let go of your inner mother and flow along in this zone, you'll have max fun and improve your riding.

Unfortunately, we can't just put on a Flow-Tron 2000 helmet and instantly feel that ecstasy. (If we could, we'd never do anything else.) According to the book *Good Stress, Bad Stress* by Barry Lenson, flow is a precise psychological state that requires these elements:

Adequate skills. You don't learn to flow. You learn to ride your bike. When you can corner, hop, and jump without thinking, then you can flow. You might achieve ecstasy in the soft Santa Cruz woods but flounder amid the raspy Phoenix boulders. When you worry about surviving the ride, you do not flow.

Goals. If you ride around—la la la—with no mission, you miss the rewards of accomplishing your goals. Set a goal. Spin smoothly, rail corners, stay on your buddy's wheel, or just stay on your bike for a change. If you need a ready-made structure, compete in a race. You have to know you're doing a good job.

Excitement. Too little stress and your mind wanders. Too much stress and you freak out. Go ahead and let some butterflies flutter in your tummy. They tell you you're being pushed, and that a huge stoke awaits.

The good news is, achieving flow is neither random nor extremely difficult. Here are some tips to help you achieve flow more consistently and in crazier situations.

Break 'em down. Break big tasks into small components. If you're an intermediate jumper and you try to nail a technical 10-pack all at once, you'll end up more broken than satisfied. Instead, try to get a perfect takeoff on the first double, then master the landing. When you get that down, add jumps number two, number three, and so on.

Practice. Don't just go out and ride, either. Pay close attention to what you're doing. Systematically build the skills you need to rip. Focus your mind on pedaling perfect circles. Then do a million of them.

Hang with the right crowd. Ride with people at or above your skill level. You will rise or fall to the level of your peers. Beware: If you feel inadequate around superior riders, or if they take you places you aren't ready for, you'll find it difficult to have a good time.

Pick the right tool for the job. You should not be worrying about your bike tracking correctly or holding together. You heard it here first: Go forth and buy!

Brian Feels the Flow

The best flow I ever had was at the 1998 World Cup downhill in Big Bear, California, in my qualifying run. This was back when Nico Vouilloz was the man (he was the man the entire time he raced). I took first and he took second. It was weird. I didn't try super hard. I had a smooth, flawless run. I didn't charge, I didn't feel like I sprinted very hard, I didn't feel super fast. Yet I beat Nico.

In the race, I tried way harder and wound up third or fourth. Despite all that extra effort, I was only like a half-second faster. Way more effort, barely anything.

Conquer your obstacles. Pay attention to the things that prevent or interrupt your flow. Maybe you tense up every time you encounter baby head rocks. Either stay away from them or learn to ride them.

Don't pay attention to yourself. As soon as you realize you're ripping, the ripping pretty much stops. Remember that scene in *Empire Strikes Back* when Luke stood on one hand with his eyes closed, with Yoda and a bunch of stuff balanced on his feet, and he started to levitate his X-wing fighter? He was definitely ripping. As soon as he opened his eyes and thought, "Yes! I'm a Jedi Master!" it all came crashing down. Don't be self-conscious like Luke. Be confident like Han.

Know Why You Ride

A lot of us ride every day. We ride and ride and ride. When we're not riding, we think about riding. But I'll bet most of us have a hard time explaining why we ride.

Is it for fun? For exercise? For a feeling of freedom? To make a living? Whatever your reasons for riding, that's cool. Just know your reasons.

When you know your motivations, you can design your path to happiness. If you just want to have some fun and burn some calories, then ride safely and enjoy your Sunday rides. If you want to make a living as a pro, then get serious about training and racing. If you need to become a great rider to validate yourself as a worthwhile person, good luck. You'll find that after you clear the jump or win the race or wax your buddies, that hole in your soul will still be there.

Shoot Your Troubles

Problem: As you zip along a trail, you get bogged down on certain obstacles; for example rocks, logs, or inflatable alligators.

Solutions: Keep your eyes moving. Notice the obstacle, then keep tracking forward. Practice the things that give you pause (and make you pause).

Problem: While your buddies fly through technical sections, you get caught in all the tight corners.

Solution: Try following a straighter line over rocks and such. The less you have to turn, the better (assuming you can get over the rocks and such).

Problem: You crash a lot.

Solution: Slow down and take mellower lines! Don't go fast and gnarly until you master slow and easy.

Problem: You slow way down in rough sections where you can't pedal.

Solution: Pump the terrain. As an exercise, see how fast you can ride without pedaling. You'll be amazed at your high speed—and your high heart rate.

Problem: You get tense in certain situations, say rock gardens or dense woods.

Solution: You're probably afraid for a reason—a crash, a scary clown, whatever. To ease your anxiety, ride these sections very slowly and strive for ultimate smoothness. Start increasing the speed after the scary clown leaves you alone.

Flow goes way beyond the mechanics of controlling a bike. It's a philosophy and a style. It's your way of experiencing the trail, of using your skills and equipment to have the most fun possible. Do you stay low and fast or fly high and stylish? Whichever your inclination, turn off your brain and let your skills come together on the fly. You'll be amazed at what you come up with.

10

Handle Crazy Conditions

Mountain biking gets its soul from the random situations you can find yourself in: steep rocks with wet moss, tangled roots covered in snow, deadly ruts lined with mud, and so on. If you want to stay sterile, ride the skate park or BMX track. If you want to go insane, hit the trail!

When the terrain gets rough, slick, and loose, it's more important than ever to stay relaxed and light on your bike, and to look where you want to go. If you promise to do that much, feel free to use these tips when the going gets weird.

Unnecessary Roughness

You never know when a rock will buck your rear wheel, so you might as well stay loose and look where you're going.

Rocks, logs, roots, ruts, and bumps can be the stuff of nightmares or they can make your dreams come true. Let's opt for the latter.

Think of a rough trail like a colossal rhythm section. The rocks, logs, roots, ruts, and bumps are merely obstacles to be handled. Depending on your speed, the roughness of the section, and the length of the section, you might roll lightly, manual, hop, jump, or go around. The key is, don't think of roughness as a threat. Think of it as a series of little obstacles that you can handle one at a time. Here are some general tips:

Carry speed. It's a big mistake to slow down too much for rough terrain. Momentum keeps you high on the bumps and carries you all the way through rough sections. Steve Peat says, "Sometimes the best thing to do is just pedal as fast as you can, get off the back of the bike and try to skim over the tops of the rocks. It's like a whoop section on a motocross track. The faster you go, the smoother it is."

Ratchet it. When you don't have enough clearance for full pedal strokes, ratchet your pedals back and forth for some propulsion action.

If it's small, fly over it. Single stones, lone logs, and small sections should get one of your patented hops or jumps. There's no good reason to run into the fronts of these guys unless you want to jump over something else.

Go light. When you reach a long series of hits that you can't absorb individually, pull your bike up into you so your tires and suspension absorb the jolts and your bike skims across the tops of the bumps. You have to be extra light when crossing a bunch of random objects—a big tangle of roots, for example. "Oh yeah, you just ping through roots," says Peat. "You gotta be loose, because you *will* get sent this way and that." Flat pedals require some downward pressure to keep you aboard; you can get way lighter with clip-in pedals.

Pump it. You can actually gain speed in rough sections that bog most riders down. The key is unweighting and weighting in the right places. All you have to do is unweight (or fly over) the front side of an object—be it a log, rock, or root—and press down on the backside. If there's a section with a bunch of little roots, you can unweight all the way through them then pump the last one for free love.

"When I get into rocks I like to get light so the bike can skim over the rocks," says Peat. "But you start to bog down after a little while, so I look for a place to pop up again." In long sections you can float over the beginning, pump in one spot, float some more, pump again, and so on. As long as your front wheel isn't hitting something while you pump the back wheel, you're golden.

Bonus: This "dive in and pump it" philosophy forces you to aim deep into the section rather than freaking out on the first obstacle. You'll carry more speed and stay smoother this way.

Free your front wheel, and the rest will follow. You'd be amazed at what your rear wheel can get over if your front wheel is already clear. If you encounter a rock, log, root, or whatever surrounded by relatively smooth ground, manual your front wheel over it, lighten the rear as it rolls over, then pump the obstacle for speed. When you enter a tangled mess of yuckiness, unweight your front tire so your rear can roll free and fast. When your front and rear wheels hit obstacles at the same time, you'll bog down like a woolly mammoth in tar. So when you enter a tangled mess of yuckiness, unweight your front tire so your rear tire can roll free and fast.

Pro downhiller Curtis Keene projects his head straight down the trail and lets his bike worry about all those pesky rocks.

You might as well jump. Trying to roll over truly rough terrain—for example, steep rocks with big holes between them—is just asking for hard hits, stuck front wheels, and over-the-bars experiences. If you have the speed, it's best to fly. Either bunny hop from flat ground or use an obstacle as an impromptu takeoff lip. Catch a little backside for a smooth landing and some free speed. Remember, never smack into the front of an obstacle unless you're using it to jump over the next obstacle.

Too Rough for Brian's Grip

Back in the day, we didn't have the bikes we have now. The World Cup downhill course in Nevegal, Italy, was so rough you could only do three runs in one day. You'd be so tired and your hands would be covered with blisters. The course was all different. It was steep and high speed, then technical singletrack with slippery roots and rocks, then ski slope at full speed with rocks in the grass, then—bam!—back into the forest with slick roots and rocks, then—bam!—high-speed ski slopes with rocks. It was hard to hold on. One year I was about a minute from the bottom on this medium-speed section. I was so tired, my hands came off the bars and I didn't make the turn. I went straight into the crowd!

© Shawn Spomer

Slippery When Wet

Bad traction is bad traction, whether you blame water, mud, ice, sand, cooking spray, or cheap tires. When your tires and the ground have trouble communicating, things are tough on the whole family. When that happens, you need some counseling:

Stay loose and ready for funny business.   "If you go in thinking, 'This is mud. I'm gonna slide around,' you're more ready when it happens," Peat says. "You can't go in thinking you'll be fine. It's mud; you won't be fine."

Keep it as straight as possible.   You can't carve turns on wet roots. Square off your turns on decent dirt and then fly straight through the nasty sections. As long as you're going straight, you don't have to go slower than normal.

Don't make any sudden moves.   The ground has trouble hearing everything when your tire talks too fast. Speak slowly and clearly, if you know what we mean, and wait for the ground to hear what you're saying.

Greg Minnaar found some mud on the 2004 national downhill course at Snowshoe, West Virginia.

Hit slick objects straight on. Hit a slimy root with an angle of incidence, and you're in for a nasty incident.

When you do encounter roots at an angle, try to pop your front wheel over them and lighten your back wheel as much as possible. "It's almost like a bunny hop, but you're not really taking off. You're just going light," Peat says. This also works when you hit things head-on.

When you're climbing in slop, stay in the saddle to keep as much weight as possible on the rear tire. As soon as you stand, you'll lose traction and momentum, and it's almost impossible to get going again on a muddy climb. Pull a taller gear than normal to dilute your power impulse and keep the tire from breaking loose.

Pick your pedaling spots. Because you can't find traction on a slick root, you need to accelerate where there's traction and carry speed over the roots.

Snow can be good or bad. According to Peat, when the top is frozen with frost, you get decent traction and roll fast. When the snow is soft, you sink down and bog. Ice is always bad news, unless you have metal spikes on your tires.

Run the right tires. Slickness calls for sticky rubber and pointy knobs. For snow and terrible mud, run spike tires.

Bonus move from Steve Peat himself: "If it's slippery and your rear end starts sliding out, lean forward to get your front wheel tracking, and the back will come back in line." This might seem counterintuitive, but Peaty knows what he's talking about.

Dealing With Slop

Where Peat lives in northern England, they have mud the way California has dust. Add all his World Cup experience, and you get a guy who knows mud riding. Peaty says you should get used to the sliding feeling and just go for it. In addition to adopting a banzai attitude, you can try a few tricks to improve your control and comfort:

- Wrap a thin, knotted rope around your grips, in case you get mud on your gloves.
- If rain is falling into your goggles or glasses, extend your visor by attaching a clear lens to the end.
- Peat runs Smith Roll-Offs in really bad weather. If water gets below the film, the film can stick to the lens. The solution: Glue loops of fishing line to your lens, to suspend the film a bit.
- When water flings forward off your tire and into your face, add a rubber flap to the front of your fender.
- Fasten a strip of tire tread to your saddle to help you translate your body English into bike English.

Brian Hates Slipperiness

I never really liked the slick roots. Coming from SoCal we don't get much rain and we have no roots. Vermont was always slippery back in the day, and so was Nevegal, Italy, with all those wet roots and slippery rock sections. To ride that stuff you gotta have good finesse and balance. You have to go with the bike and not fight it. That doesn't suit my style. I like to be in control at all times. In that stuff you gotta be willing to be out of control and just go with it.

Soft, Deep, and Loose

Deep sand, dust, gravel, mud, and snow all have a way of mucking up your cornering and bogging you to a sketchy stop. Give those jerks the treatment:

Find a balance point somewhere near the back of your bike. Weight your front wheel enough so it tracks straight and grabs when you turn the bars, but not so much that it sinks in and scrubs your speed. If you've skied powder, you already have a feel for this: Lean forward enough to control your skis but not so much the tips dive into the snow.

If you hit a patch of sand while you're going fast, lean back and unweight your front wheel *before* your bike starts to slow down. Keep that front end light and motor across like a floatplane lifting skyward.

Climbing in looseness is like climbing in slipperiness. Keep your bum on the seat and make smooth power. Spin an easier gear than normal so you don't bog down.

Cornering in loose dust is like trying to steer a cargo ship. You can do it, but your vessel doesn't respond very quickly. Turn your bars slowly and wait for your bike to come around. If you steer too much too soon, your front wheel will plow, which is just like sliding out except your tire usually catches traction and pitches you forward.

Braking in looseness requires an ultra-light touch, especially in front. Make sure your bike is upright. Get back and low to get more out of your rear brake. And ease off the front binder at the first sign of plowage. Now the good news: Deep snow, sand, and mud all like to scrub your speed, so you don't have to brake as much as you would on hardpack. (When you ski down the fall line through deep powder, the snow controls your speed. Same kind of thing.)

It's all the same. You swim through dust, you wiggle on gravel, and you ping off baby-head rocks. The symptoms seem different but the treatment is identical: Stay loose and expect your bike to act like an idiot.

Cut this out and stick it to your refrigerator: As long as your body stays on track, it doesn't matter what your bike is doing.

A skidding rear tire and a free-rolling front tire make this Whistler scree slope seem easy. Not.

Getting Loose on the Kamikaze

The Kamikaze Downhill at Mammoth Mountain was made of ground pumice, and it was always dusty and loose. You could get going so fast—up to around 60 miles per hour—any sudden movement or jerk was disastrous. The good line was bad enough, but when you got off the main line it was even deeper and looser. You had to stay light on your bike and let both tires drift through the turns.

Avoiding the Rut

Running water and rolling tires can carve mini-canyons into your favorite trails. These wheel trappers mess up your balance, scrub your speed, and collect rocks and other nasties. They're usually to be avoided, but they can be your friends.

Ruts can be your enemies or your friends. This one is definitely a friend. Todd Bosch pulls some major g's. Note his complete lack of braking.

Stay out of rain ruts.   Ruts that run down the trail love to grab you and lead you into terrible situations. On a fire road or doubletrack, there's plenty of room to take a better line. If the trail is super narrow and there's nowhere else to ride, go ahead and take the rut. Use your rear brake to control your speed. Front braking always ruins steering; ruts make it worse.

Stay out of uphill ruts.   When you climb in a rut and your rear tire scrubs the canyon wall, you lose speed and risk a slide-out. That's if your pedal doesn't smash into the ground first. Climb above the ruts. If your back tire does slide down in there, keep pedaling and get out as soon as you can.

Stay out of narrow ruts.   Narrow ruts keep you from wiggling around for balance. Paradoxically, the faster you go through a narrow rut, the better.

Cross ruts with caution.   When you have to cross a rut, try to hit it at an angle, and don't let your tires get caught in there. If you hit a small rut head-on, you can just get light on your bike. If you need to span a huge rut that runs parallel to your travel, hop over the entire thing. Manualing works for smooth transitions, but if the transition is smooth you won't be worrying about the rut, will you?

Use ruts in turns.   When hundreds of riders have carved through a soft corner, the best line gets crammed several inches into the earth, and it makes a fantastic berm—especially on flat or off-camber corners. When the ruts get deeper than six inches or they develop big holes, they become a hazard. Find a different line.

When the going gets precarious, keep those eyes forward.

Riding the Skinnies

Bridges sprouted up in the North Vancouver woods as a way for riders to ride over heavy foliage and deep sogginess. As riders got better at clinging to the log-and-lumber structures, the bridges ceased being practical ways to traverse unrideable terrain and became a focal point for a whole new style of riding: part cross-country and part downhill, but mostly trials. Nowadays, freeriders roll 15 feet above the forest floor on four-inch-wide logs. No wonder these "bridges" are now called skinnies.

Skinnies range from burly lumber ladders to spindly soggy branches, and heights range from less than a foot to 20 feet or more. Technically, skinnies are no harder to ride than any other narrow line, such as a thin rut or a tiny rock takeoff. Skinnies just look scarier and carry a higher price for error. If you learn to ride skinnies, you'll be able to flow nicely on modern freeride trails and you'll become a master of balance and pinpoint line control. Just remember:

It's all mental.   You can easily ride the white stripe at 20 miles per hour, but put a 2-by-6 a few feet off the ground, and you forget how to ride. Remember that your tires only need a few inches of surface; the rest is just decoration.

Look as far forward as possible.   Aim where you want to go, for all the typical reasons. This is easier said than done, but you must not look at your front tire. Doing so leads to the dreaded low-speed wobble, which leads to sudden vertical acceleration—and sudden deceleration.

Momentum is your friend.   Ride the white stripe at 20 miles per hour, then try it at 2 miles per hour. Harder, eh?

Run a taller gear than normal.   Spinning a low gear makes you feel all lumpy and out of control. Turn a harder gear for a more controlled burst up that slimy ladder. You'll maintain better balance, and you're less likely to burn out on that green moss.

Careful in the turns.   As you round a bend to transfer to an even skinnier bridge, turn your front tire out wide so your rear can track inside without falling into oblivion. Top-notch skinnies have little platforms for just this purpose. To keep max rubber on the tree, keep your bike upright and lean with your body.

Run big, sticky tires.   Lower your pressure for dedicated skinny sessions, but beware pinch flats when you drop onto rocks.

Choose your exit.   Like we said, riding a skinny bridge is just like riding any other skinny line—until you get off line. If you start veering to the side and you're close to clean ground, just ride off and drop to safety. If you experience a balance blowout close to a smooth surface, ditch the bike and land on your feet. When you're suspended way above gnarl, jettison your steed and hug the bridge.

Start wide and low.   Lay a piece of lumber on the ground and ride it. When you get a 2-by-8 dialed, step up (down?) to a 2-by-4. When you can stay on that as long as you want, try elevating it a bit at a time. Like we said, most of skinny riding is mental. Build your confidence gradually. Never put yourself into a situation where you freak out a dozen feet above pointy rocks. Not cool.

Brandon Sloan of Specialized tests one of his creations on Vancouver's North Shore.

Thanks to Brandon Sloan for sharing his tips. Sloan is the product manager for Specialized's freeride bikes, and he schools most of the North Shore crew when he goes up there to test his new weapons.

Shoot Your Troubles

Problem: You feel like you're getting beaten to death on rough terrain.

Solutions: Make sure your bike is set up correctly. Loosen your grip and relax your upper body. Look ahead. Load the bike in smooth sections and unload the bike in rough sections.

Problem: On rough terrain, you feel like you're balling up and getting stuck.

Solutions: Go faster. Unweight your bike, especially your front end, when you encounter obstacles.

Problem: When the going gets slick and loose, you feel like a sick goose.

Solution: This is pretty philosophical. When the ground sticks as well as a nonstick pan coated in cooking spray, you have to be willing to be out of control and go with it. That sounds pretty nutty, but that's the way it is. Wear pads if that helps your confidence.

Problem: On loose ground, your front wheel digs in and pushes the dirt. Sometimes it catches and pitches you forward.

Solution: Your weight is too far forward. Move back a bit, with more weight on your feet and less weight on your hands.

Problem: On loose ground, your front wheel skims over the surface and refuses to steer.

Solution: Your weight is too far back. Move forward a bit with more pressure on your hands.

Problem: You have trouble holding a line, whether it's between two ghastly ruts or atop an elevated 2-by-4.

Solution: Stay loose and look where you want to go (as always). Remember that a little momentum will carry you through a situation faster than you can worry about that situation.

Problem: As you go down rough terrain, your bike feels like it won't move around. You feel like you're getting pitched forward. It's hard to lean into turns.

Solution: Your thighs might be interfering with the movement of your saddle. Spread your knees apart to let your bike bounce around and pitch into corners. Try lowering your seat.

Brian Decides to Get Skinny

When I rode in Whistler the first time, I was kind of sketched out by all the little bridges on the A River Runs Through It trail and on some of the downhill trails. I'd never done that kind of riding, you know, so I was being really cautious at first. But once I tried a few, they were fun.

When Dangerous Dan Cowan was in my area doing his freeride show, he left me all his wooden stunts, and a bunch of friends and I installed them in my backyard. None of my skinnies are too skinny—maybe four to five inches wide, but they're a cool challenge, something different, a new side of mountain biking. Even though I'll probably never race on something like that (but who knows?), it's all about pushing your limits and building confidence in different situations. You want to be a well-rounded rider. You don't want to go on a ride with friends one day and be the only one to walk over the bridge.

Teeters require the balance of skinnies, plus perfect timing. The smaller the teeter, the smaller your error margin.

Problem: You get beaten up while trying to pedal over rough terrain.

Solution: Get off the saddle, even if only a fraction of an inch. Put all your weight on your pedals and let your bike react to impacts. For lots of rough pedaling, lower your seat a quarter-inch or so to give yourself more room to work. For more powerful pedaling on relatively smooth sections, slide back on your saddle. This will approximate your normal height.

Crazy conditions have a way of freaking out riders who aren't used to them. Bury a southern Californian in deep mud, and he'll wig out. Slide an East Coaster on a hardpacked fire road and she'll feel sketched. Although these conditions might seem strange and different, they have a lot in common: You should stay loose, look where you're going, and have fun!

11

Race Like a Champ

© Shawn Spomer

Racing is just like riding, only it's for keeps. On race day you need all your play-day skills, plus a few special tricks to give you an extra edge.

Strengthen Your Mind

In any competitive class, a handful of people have the physical strength and skills to win. To win, you need the emotional and mental skills to hold it together throughout the race. Here are some tips to make you as stony as a statue.

Race for the Right Reasons

Racing is just like riding, only a result sheet tells you exactly where you rank. Competition can stoke you out and inspire you to new greatness, or it can bum you out and spoil you on riding. The determining factor isn't whether you win or lose the race; it's how you perform in relation to your expectations and goals. We enter races for myriad reasons: to wield our powers against others; to see how we stand against the best; to make a living; to challenge ourselves; to ride as fast as we want on fun courses; to travel to cool places; to bash elbows with our buddies; to commune with the racing tribe; to validate the time, money, and energy we put into our sport; and, for some of us, to validate ourselves as riders and as people. Before you reach the starting line, take the time to figure out what, exactly, you expect to get from the experience. By setting clear expectations, you'll know what to strive for, and you'll know how to measure your success. Here are some things to keep in mind:

Why **is more powerful than** *what.* Think about the reasons you race. Whether you race for self-improvement (good reason) or to destroy other people (not such a good reason), your fundamental goal will drive you through the inevitable difficulties—and successes.

Enjoy the process. Riding (and living) is a never-ending process of increasing your strength and skills. When you become serious about racing, you dedicate yourself to the process of finishing higher and higher in more challenging events and, eventually, in higher classes. Just as learning to jump a 10-foot double is a step on the way to jumping a 12-footer, then a 15-footer, and on and on until the requirements outweigh the rewards, earning 87th place is a step toward 10th place, then 3rd, then 1st, and then up to a harder class. Write down your racing goals and keep track of your progress. When you feel defeated or question your motives, your racing log will keep you

Racing is 90 percent physical. The other 90 percent is mental. Put Billy Owczarski on a race course, and he's all business.

motivated. Remember: Keep striving to improve, but enjoy where you are and take the time to appreciate what you've already accomplished.

Remember: It's only bike racing.   What? Blasphemy! After you strip away your ego, winning a race means only this: You were the fastest or first rider on that day, in those conditions, among that group of racers. Anything—different terrain, weather, racers, or luck—could have dropped you to number two. Shoot, if you were in a higher class, you might have been in 87th! In racing (and in life) you can control only yourself—and then sometimes only barely. Try not to worry about things that are outside your control. If someone flats and you move up a spot, don't be too proud of yourself. In the same way, if a competitor makes a clever move and you fall a spot, don't be too bummed.

If you believe the old No Fear T-shirt that said, "Second place is the first loser," you are in for a world of pain.

Have reasonable expectations.   The most reasonable expectation is, "I will do my best," whatever that means to you. For most people, the most unreasonable expectation is, "I will win." If you expect to win all the time, expect to be disappointed much of the time. In a time-trial event, you have no influence on other people's runs. If they are fitter, better skilled, more clever, or ride in faster conditions, they might beat you. Do everything you can to ensure a good time, but in the end realize that times are what they are: just times. Racing head-to-head is even more complicated. You can get beaten because of a crash, a clever pass, superior fitness, or mental toughness. Win or no win, either way, do your best.

The next time you get too serious during practice, remember that racing is a great opportunity to goof off with your bros.

Don't Let a Bad Result Ruin a Good Time

I (Lee) have been completely stoked on a race run and then been devastated when the results ranked me lower than I wanted to be. What a shame, to let my placing ruin a good time. On the other end, I've completely blown race runs and then been jazzed when the results showed everyone else blew it worse. How shallow, to take pleasure in other people's catastrophes. Both extremes—letting a bad result ruin a great race and letting a good result erase a bad race—show a lack of internal goals. Not only will this not help you improve, it's also no fun.

Set personal performance goals.   As we've been saying, "winning" is arbitrary and, in large part, out of your control. Set goals for yourself: In a downhill, lay off your brakes through the tricky rock section; in a cross-country, maintain 176 beats per minute on the climbs; in a bikercross, don't let anyone low–high you. Whether you win or not, judge yourself by how well you met your goals. But keep in mind that this is racing. Keep striving to do better. Otherwise, go for a fun ride and save the entry fee.

Pick the right class.   Racing is a great opportunity to compare yourself with other riders of the same caliber. The best racing class for you depends on your reasons for racing. If you want a challenge, race in a class that lets you ride fun courses with riders who will push you. For the most intense competition, race in a class that you have a chance, but no guarantee, of winning. There's nothing as exciting as battling it out with close competitors. "Losing" makes you hungry, and "winning" is definitely something to be proud of. If you must destroy other people to feel good about yourself, go ahead and stay in an easy class. Enjoy your five overall titles in Beginner 30-34, then move on to destroy Beginner 35-39. But be warned: There is a special hell for sandbaggers, and your competitors will try to send you there.

Use your losses.   You can always go faster. Learn from your mistakes. In a way, second place is more exciting than first place. When you win, you feel good and there are no excuses, but you start wondering about where to go from there. When you take a close 2nd (or 3rd or 87th or whatever), you get really hungry and hypermotivated to do better next time. The drive toward improvement is much more powerful than the satisfaction of accomplishment.

Get Into the Racing Zone

You've heard all types of competitors talk about getting into "the zone." The zone is like the state of flow (chapter 9), only it's more intense. You've blocked out everything but what you need to win the race. There are good riders—people who flow smoothly while they're out playing with their buddies, but who crumble under pressure—and there are good racers—those who can reach the zone and drop the hammer on command. Here are some tips to help you reach the racing zone.

Visualize

This is the key to a great performance. Imagine yourself having a great race. Fill in as much detail as you can—sights, sounds, sensations. Run your race in real time. Imagine what you'll do if you get off line or get passed. If you imagine something in enough detail, it's as if your brain is practicing in real life.

Before the start of the 1993 Mammoth Kamikaze, Missy Giove sat by herself on a rock outcropping, pedaling with her hands and leaning into each corner, imagining every detail of the racecourse. The phrase "If you can see it, you can be it" is usually true. The phrase "If you can't see it, you can't be it" is always true.

Why Do You Race?
How Have Your Reasons Changed Over the Years?

Lee

In the beginning I raced to prove myself as a good bike rider. I'd never been competitive in any sport, and the podium seemed like such a glorious place, a place for studly people (I saw myself as an overweight wimp). After a few years, the need to win started taking over. I focused on downhill, finally won a Sport race, and jumped to Expert. I really thought I'd win races and go pro. At a very deep level, I needed to win in order to feel good about myself. Second place made me angry. Around this time, I stopped having fun.

After I suffered a concussion in a downhill, I took a break from racing. Once I relaxed, my skills grew like crazy and I started having fun again. I tried a race in late 2001, just for kicks, and won it. Then I goofed off at another race and won that one, too. In late 2001 and 2002, I raced 20 times and won eight times in Expert. I wasn't really training; I just showed up and relied on the skills and fitness I'd gained from playing. I was enjoying the scene, the competition, and my ever-increasing skills. In 2003, I set the goal of winning a national. I quit my day job to focus on riding and writing, and I rode just about every day with fast pros. We trained extremely hard—distance, intervals, the whole thing. My skills and strength jumped dramatically, but I was so intense I couldn't find my flow, and I wound up blowing all the nationals. I went into 2004 hoping to have faith in my abilities and to let the results take care of themselves—and it seems to have worked. I won the Expert downhills at the Sea Otter Classic and the Durango national, and I ended the year as the top-ranked American Expert downhiller in my age group. In 2005 I plan to race semipro downhill. My days of winning are probably over, but my days of improving have just begun.

Mark Weir

(Pro cross-country and downhill racer, as well as the public relations face for WTB)

At first it was to test myself and to see what I could do. I was into being a national champion, being one of the best in the world.

But I'm not willing to give up family time, time with my girl, to travel all over the place. Maybe I have the talent and drive to be a champion at something. But I want have fun, to ride my bike with my buddies. I love grassroots racing, especially here in NorCal. We have more participants than the nationals. We're having fun, hanging out with our friends.

Racing is only 30 percent of how a guy like me makes a living. I try to get press for WTB, hang out with cool people, do some PR. I find events that the media embrace. The nationals are boring. But the Cascade Cream Puff 100, battling the 24-hour championships on singlespeeds, a downhiller racing pro cross-country, that all gets coverage.

I just want to do what I want to do. I hope it doesn't end.

Brian

Well, I have a house to pay for . . .

No, actually, I love winning and I love riding my bike. I'm lucky enough to get paid to do it. If I didn't race, I'd still ride. It's all I know how to do; I've been doing it since I was four and a half. That's my life—bikes.

Beginner-Class Drama With Lee

It was my second race ever, a cross-country in San Bernardino, California. In my first race, my wimpy climbing and pantywaist descending had gotten me waxed, and I'd vowed to come back stronger and tougher. To give you an idea of how long ago this was, I rode a 1989 Diamondback Apex, powder-coated fluorescent pink, and I wore a pink helmet cover and a pink long-sleeved top—and I was stylin'. The race was very hard, but I stayed in front on the climbs, and I held it together on the descents. As I approached the finish in first place, I came upon a huge, scary puddle. As I rode around it, a dude splashed straight through, passed me, and finished ahead of me. The organizer said Mr. Splash was in a different age group and gave me first place. Stoked! I'd won my second race ever! I felt unbelievably awesome. Later, I went to the booth for a T-shirt to commemorate my great day. The announcer said, "Oh, we're glad you're still here. The guy who passed you *was* in your class. We need that first-place medal back." I was crushed. First place seemed so glorious. Second felt so terrible. In hindsight, I was being silly. I'd put in a fine performance with two different results and two very different feelings. I should have been less concerned with the color of my medal and more concerned with how I did: I climbed and descended like a champ—but next time I'll go straight through the puddle.

Focus, But in a Relaxed Way

When your Stanford MBA left brain starts to chatter about race pressure, the huge jump, or whatever, it's time to wake up your Berkeley hippie right brain and chill out. To quiet the inner Republican, try focusing on your breathing. Bring air deeply and easily into your belly, and focus on your center, right behind your belly button. This sounds all new-age hippie-dippy, but it really works. You will feel the nervous energy leave your noggin and settle comfortably in your core. Use this to focus before your event, and try it when you're pedaling so hard the entire universe consists of pain. Here are some other things to keep in mind—well, not really *in* mind 'cause that would be a distraction:

- Keep your mind quiet, with no extraneous thoughts whatsoever.
- Think positively and don't let negative thoughts distract you.
- Relax and let your body and mind do what they know how to do.
- If you're having a great race, don't let the catastrophic "Hey, I'm gonna win" thought enter your mind. It's hard to keep those thoughts out, but you must. Concentrate all your energy on finishing the race.

Follow Your Prerace Routine

Do you remember the way you felt the last time you had a great race? Do whatever it takes to get into that same place. Eat your special dinner, get your sleep, practice in the morning, check every bolt on your bike, take a nap, wear mismatched socks, warm up with your ThighMaster, or whatever. Your prerace routine is a ladder you climb to your peak performance. Your racing gear—jersey, armor, shoes, or whatever—can help you get that extra eye of the tiger.

Your routine should be flexible enough to withstand sharing a condo with 19 guys, but your warm-up and the last few minutes before your race should be sacred. Do whatever you need to feel warm, relaxed, and centered.

Right before the race, some guys vent nervous energy by goofing around, while others prefer to separate themselves from the frenzy. A lot of guys joke around and stuff, but I (Brian) keep to myself and concentrate on what I have to do. Steve Blick, my Oakley rep, is one of my best friends, but I don't even talk to him up on the start line. I just hand him my dirty glasses and he hands me clean ones. We hang out and party after the race.

> ### Racing for External Validation, Lee McCormack
>
> Once I realized I was racing to somehow validate myself as a person, I started entering "External Validation" as my sponsor on my entry form. When I won a race, the announcer would say, "And in first place, riding for External Validation . . . ."

Don't Spaz Out

Many beginning racers get too excited and they lose their minds on race day. After five perfect practice runs, they'll fall in the first corner, pedal too hard to make up time, blow up, fall again, and then forget where they left their car keys.

Don't put too much pressure on yourself. If 1 is sleep and 10 is panic, shoot for an 8 or 9. Remember: This is just a bike ride. With results. And series points. And sponsorship on the line. . . . Oops, sorry. Just chill out and have fun.

Don't Let Mistakes Freak You Out

Some tennis players symbolically wipe their mistakes off their rackets before they continue their game. Maybe you could wipe your mistakes off your handlebar. No matter where you wipe them, you have to get over your mistakes and get back onto your race plan. Don't go nuts trying to make up for lost time, either. Stay within your abilities, and everything will go as well as it's supposed to.

Remind Yourself With Keywords

Pick a word that encapsulates what you're trying to do and say it to yourself to keep you focused. "Spin" might help you climb efficiently. "Float" might carry you over a rock garden. "Bam!" might help you holeshot a World Cup 4X . . . but probably not.

Listen to Tunes

Music has a powerful ability to shape our thoughts. If you need to relax, go for some Kenny G. If you need to get amped up, crank up Metallica's *Frantic*.

Brian's Unbeatable Confidence

One of the keys to my racing success is confidence. When I get into the start gate, I know I'm the man to beat, that the other guys are worrying about how to beat me.

When you're winning, you're not worried about little things and other people—"I gotta get a good start, cut that guy off, do this and that." You have no doubts. You get in the gate, and you know you've won the past couple races, so it's just a matter of doing it again. You know how to do it, and you just do it. It's a great thing.

But it can work against you if you get too nonchalant. When you get a little cocky, you take things for granted, and maybe you don't go as hard as you should.

Bikercross

In bikercross (aka mountain cross and 4X), four racers blast out of a steel gate and race down a course with humps, jumps, berms, and flat turns. The runs last about 30 seconds. To qualify, each rider runs an individual time trial. Depending on the size of the race, the fastest 4, 8, 16, 32, or 64 riders advance to the finals. The fastest two are pitted against the slowest two, the next fastest two are matched with the next slowest two, and so on until all the brackets are filled. Following each heat, the two fastest riders advance to the next round, while the other two become spectators. This continues until only four are left and the winners cross the line.

To excel in bikercross, racers need good all-around bike skills—explosive pedaling, confident jumping, clean cornering—plus fast starts, decisive passing, and clever tactics. In bikercross, sometimes the winner isn't the fastest rider—it's the smartest rider.

Start Like a Bullet

Many bikercross races are won on the starting line. If you get the hole shot, there's a strong chance you'll hold the pack at bay and win the race. If you come out last, you have to work your way through some ferocious traffic. So work on those starts!

Choose the Right Lane

Lane choice can make or break a race. The fastest qualifiers get the first lane choice. Since you're reading this book, we know you'll be qualifying fast, and you'll have to deal with this situation.

The shortest route to the first corner usually wins. On most courses, this is lane one. Of course, there are exceptions.

© Shawn Spomer

Brian Schmith, Brian Lopes, Cedric Gracia, and Eric Carter hammer down the first straight in Kamloops, British Columbia.

Sometimes lane one is so far inside that you have to swing into lane two to enter the first turn. If the lane two rider is right there, you have to slow down—"shut down"—and let him in first. Not cool. Next time pick lane two.

Know your competitors' strengths. Just because you qualified first doesn't make you the fastest starter. If you think you'll get beaten to the first turn, line up on the outside rather than the inside. If you get shut down in lane one, you have to slow down and let everyone go by. If you get beaten in lane four, you can follow with speed and stay in the game.

Be sure to look at the course. Maybe the first jump is faster on the outside lane, or maybe there's a mud puddle on the inside lane. And this one seems obvious, but it's important: Make sure your gate is clear of rocks, sand, mud, or anything else that can slow you down.

Lopes Lane Choice in Action

At the Vermont national bikercross in 2002, I had the first lane choice in every run because I qualified first. If you were in lane one, the chances of a shutdown were good. Wade Bootes and I were in the semi. I took lane two, and he took lane one. I snapped him out of the gate and he got balled up in the first turn and wound up not qualifying. If he had chosen lane three, he could have made it.

Choose the Right Gear

As always, you want a gear that's not so hard you bog down and not so easy you spin out and have to shift right away. Gear choice depends on the grade and the length of the runout. When in doubt, choose a low gear that gets you out front right away. The faster you can spin, the more speed you'll achieve before you have to shift. For example, a racer who turns a 34x19 gear to 80 rpm has to back off the pressure and shift at 11 mph. A competitor who can whip up to 120 rpm will reach almost 17 mph in the same gear. In an event that's won by fractions of seconds, that's a huge difference.

You should be able to achieve your optimum cadence in just a few strokes. If you're struggling to tach up, you're wasting time.

Position Your Pedals for Power

Start with your strongest foot forward, with your pedal around 2 o'clock. In a flat gate, run the pedal closer to 3 o'clock for ultimate impulse power. On a steep gate, run the pedal closer to 1:30 to carry you farther down the slope.

Traditional Gate Start

For those of you who came to bikercross from cross-country and downhill, BMX-style gates seem like crazy contraptions. You press your front wheel against a metal gate, put both feet on the pedals, and balance while you wait for the cadence. In the UCI and NBL, the cadence goes like this:

"Okay, riders, let's set 'em up."

"On the gate."

"Riders ready."

"Watch the lights."

"Beep—beep—BEEP!" and the gate drops.

Rush It

If I (Brian) am breathing hard after a run, I know the other guys must be hurting. I try to rush them into the gate before they can recover.

Time the cadence so you start pedaling *before* the gate drops. Air-driven NBL gates drop immediately out of your way. Local-style gravity-driven gates drop so slowly you can lose a half second waiting for them to drop. Just pedal right over 'em. Braaap!

Here's how to handle a traditional NBL-style gate:

1. When the command starts, stand up. You should be back on the bike, with your arms straight. You need to decide ahead of time when to take off. It's a two-step process.

2. At your first cue, start moving your body forward to create some momentum. As you pull your body forward your bike will roll back a bit. That's OK.

3. Just before the gate drops, snap! Pull as hard as you can on your bars and push as hard as you can on your pedal. This should be one huge explosion of muscle and ferocity.

4. Drive your front wheel over the gate as it drops.

5. Sprint like your entire race depends on this, which it does.

Wheelying off the line looks cool, but you want to go forward, not up. When you pull the bars and accelerate, make sure your weight is forward and the front end stays low.

The Slingshot

I (Brian) have been racing my whole life, and I've been starting the same way the entire time. While I was injured and not racing in 2003, I started practicing the slingshot. With the slingshot, you rock backward just before the gate drops and give yourself a little rolling start. I have a strong second and third pedal, but my first pedal isn't the strongest. For me, the slingshot is extremely effective. The timing is tricky, though.

1. Stand straight up or a little forward. Run your pedal a little lower than normal. You'll be rolling back a couple of inches and your pedal will come up. Make sure your chain line is straight. You don't want the links coming off your cog when you roll backward.

2. Just before the gate drops, rock your body and bike backward. Note how the pedal comes up a bit.

3. Explode! Drive your hips forward. Push on the pedals and pull on the bars.

4. Keep driving as the gate drops.

5. By the time the gate hits the ground you'll have a full head of steam.

At first it might look like the other racers are beating you off the line, but when you reach the gate you'll already have speed, and you will destroy them.

Random Gates

At NORBA nationals, the starter gives a warning and the gate drops any time within seven seconds. These gates were adopted to give mountain bikers a fair chance against BMXers, who have all done thousands of starts to that familiar NBL cadence. The gate could go right away, or it could go in seven seconds (which feels like 30 seconds when you're balancing there on the gate). Run an easy gear for a great first pedal.

1. When you get the warning stand forward. Pull on the bars and push on your power pedal. You are a coiled spring just waiting to be released!

2. When the gate drops you'll automatically spurt forward.

3. Drive your hips forward and put the power down. Push with your legs, pull with your arms, yadda, yadda, yadda.

The First Straight

When four competitors leave the gate and there's only one good line into the first turn, they politely get in line according to their qualifying times. Not! Racers blast off the line and roar forward with the intensity of a freight train. It's one of the most exciting moments in bike racing.

Focus all your energy forward. Look forward, hold your line, and stay straight. Don't go veering this way or that, and don't look at the racers next to you. If you do, you'll unconsciously slow down for a better look. Remember, you are a hurtling juggernaut of the forward type.

Follow up that snap. Your second and third pedals are almost as important as your first. When you snap downward, pull the other foot forward for that second stroke.

Pointy elbows. When I (Brian) raced pro BMX, I was one of the smallest guys out there—but I had the sharpest elbows. If a competitor creeps up on you, work your elbow into the crook of his arm and pull him backward. Physical contact like this isn't exactly legal, but it isn't exactly illegal either. At national races, many a high-level mountain biker has been juked by this old BMXer trick.

Assert yourself. If you're even slightly ahead, move toward the good line. A lot of guys are intimidated by the closeness. Hold your course, and maybe they'll back down. If not, too bad. Wear your pads just in case.

Be patient. If you get beaten into the first corner, back off. Instead of risking a nasty tangle, start planning your pass.

Passing

The back-and-forth of changing leads makes bikercross exciting to watch and even more exciting to race. You take all the physical and emotional skills needed to haul ass down a tricky course and add three other racers, each scheming for the lead. In bikercross, the action is fast and places change in an instant.

Here are some general passing tips, along with the two main types of passes:

Do your recon.　Each track has a few good passing spots. Look for places where you carry lots of speed into corners, places where you carry lots of speed out of corners, and places where you ride faster than everyone else.

Plan ahead.　Watch the other racers to see their lines and where they're fast and slow. Plan what might happen—"If I'm behind here, I'll rail the outside of this turn, carry speed out, and then pass on the rhythm" or whatever. The more thinking you do ahead of time, the more quickly you can act in the heat of battle.

Stay ready.　Don't be a sheep. Be spontaneous, creative, and devious.

Here's a classic low–high pass, as executed by amateurs at the 2004 Sea Otter Classic.

Qualifying Versus Racing

In qualifying, do whatever it takes to get down the course as fast as possible. Take the fastest lines without worrying about passing. If you can, on rough courses run a dual suspension bike for maximum overall speed and a fast qualifying time, and then race a hardtail so you can start fast and control the race from the front.

Don't follow. You can't get by someone when you're right behind him. You can't see or react, and you certainly can't ride straight through him (unless you're Wade Bootes). Hang back a bit or take a different line. Accelerate before you reach your passing point, then shoot on past.

If you can outpedal, outpump, or outjump someone on a straight section, that's fantastic. But for the most part, passing happens in corners. There are two basic approaches:

○ **High–low pass.** If the leaders dive into the inside of a berm, stay high. As they drift upward and slow down on the exit, drop down and accelerate for a pass.

This works best in a berm, but the same idea applies for flat turns. In general, the faster you dive into the inside, the more speed you end up scrubbing on the exit. By being patient, you can set up wider and later and drive out of the turn while the other goofballs struggle for traction.

○ **Low–high pass.** When the leaders sweep outside to rail a berm, dive inside. But don't blow by and drift high on the exit, or they'll high–low you. Instead, get next to them, squeeze them toward the top of the berm, and gain speed on the exit.

High–low pass

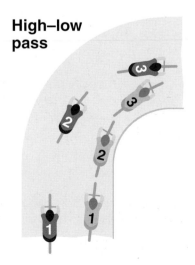

Low–high pass

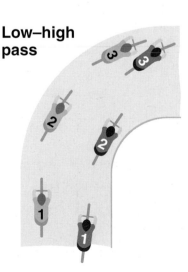

Brian's World Championship Low–High Pass

At the UCI 4X World Championship in 2002, I qualified first and I picked the inside gate in the final. I got a bad start, and Eric Carter and Michal Prokop were ahead going into the first turn. But they left a small hole for me to squeeze into. I took the hole, pushed them up high, and never looked back.

This works really well on flat corners. While you're squeezing a racer to the outside, you're in control. When you decide to sprint for the next corner, you usually have a slight head start. When you bust out a low–high pass, watch out for someone trying to high–low you from behind.

Keep it clean. A little contact is okay, but don't ram into someone on purpose. In general, if you're in front, you can push a rider behind you to the side. If you're in back, you have to find a way past. T-boning someone is not cool. There's a fine line between a clean pass and dirty racing. If you do pull a dirty pass, it'll come back to you eventually.

Preventing Passes

Sometimes you don't know someone's right behind you until he flies past, but most of the time you can feel him. If you're still in front, cut him off. If he's already caught up with you or is ahead of you, let him go and start planning your counterattack. If a guy low–highs you, hit him with the ol' high–low.

Know the good passing spots and think through the possibilities so you're ready for anything. Learn two lines for any mountain-cross race: your qualifying line, which is the fastest way down the course, and your race-leading line, which will pinch all the corners and prevent racers from barging in on you. If the qualifying and racing are done on different days, practice your qualifying line on qualifying day and practice your various race lines on race day. If you have a really clever idea, don't reveal it until your final run.

Pay attention to where the other racers are and plan your lines accordingly. They might react to you and change their plans, but if you know where they are, at least you have a chance to counterreact. In time, you'll develop a sense for these things. Until then, you might want to run a helmet mirror and maybe even some handlebar mirrors. These really help you keep tabs on your competition.

Practice These Skills

If you want to improve your bikercross performance, here are some specific things to work on:

Starts. This is huge. Go to the BMX track, buy a year's membership for $40 or so, and then show up for practice sessions. For about a buck, you can sprint your brains out for an hour and a half, which is plenty of time. Remember that quality is more important than quantity. Try to do 10 good starts per session. Blast the first straight, then pull off to recover for the next gate. If you feel strong after your start practice, try some full-lap intervals.

Jumps. Carry maximum speed over jumps. Stay low. Work on bigger jumps and different lips so you don't get caught off guard at the races.

Rhythms. Dirt-jumper doubles are good for learning to pump transitions, but you need a long set of rolling humps like you find at most BMX tracks. Practice them every which way—doubling them up, manualing, any combination you can think of. Go as fast as you can.

Berms. Get the hang of going very fast with your tires above your face. Get on the gas as early as possible. Practice low–high and high–low lines. Even better: Dice with your friends.

Flat turns. You can get great practice on any old fire road. For a real challenge, throw some cones out on a dirt lot and race your buddies. Carry max speed through a variety of lines, then sprint back up to speed as quickly as you can.

You can practice all of these skills in your car on public roads. Hard acceleration, late braking, forced passing, cutting people off . . .

Intensity. Go as hard as you possibly can for 30 seconds at a time, followed by rest and a few repeats. Intervals on a trainer or the road are brutal. Intervals on actual terrain are brutal too, but at least they're fun.

Fuel Up

On the day of the finals, let's hope you'll have an hour of practice followed by round after round of grueling racing action. You might be out there for hours, so make sure you bring food and drinks. Nothing that'll weigh you down; just enough to stay sharp. Maybe some water and Cytomax. Don't bring beer with you—that's just admitting you'll be a spectator soon.

Downhill

"30 seconds"

You lean on the start ramp.

"20 seconds"

You click into your pedals.

"10 seconds"

You adjust your goggles.

"Five . . ."

You stand.

"Four . . ."

You lean back.

"Three . . ."

Deep breath.

"Two . . ."

Okay.

"One . . ."

Your mind goes silent.

"Go!"

Your body erupts. Pedal, pedal, pedal, turn, turn, turn. Over the rocks, down the chute, off the drop. Heart pounding, lungs gasping, legs churning, you fly down the course you have etched in your memory. Here's that rock, take the inside line here. You ride the fine edge between control and catastrophe, victory and violence.

There are as many different kinds of downhill as there are mountains. Most races are two to five minutes long, but a few, like the Downieville Downhill, run up to an hour or longer. Terrain varies from easy and fast to gnarly and slow to gnarly and fast. Top downhillers possess quick reflexes, otherworldly bike-handling skills, total-body strength, and a mix of anaerobic and aerobic fitness. A certain amount of confidence doesn't hurt either.

Here are some tips to help you dominate your next downhill race.

Learn the Course

Downhill racing is just like normal trail riding, except you get to memorize the course and go as fast as you want. The better you know the course, the faster you can go. At most races you have limited time (and energy) to learn the course, so getting effective practice is important. Here's some advice from World Cup champion downhiller Steve Peat.

Walk the course before you ride it. Don't try to memorize every rock, but definitely get the overall layout. Figure out how you'll handle the tricky sections, and imagine yourself riding the course. Don't waste a short, crowded practice session checking out the course for the first time. If you formulate a plan while you walk the course, you'll be able to ride faster sooner.

Get lots of practice runs. Peat usually gets six to seven runs on day one of practice, four to five on day two, and two runs on race day. Be sure to learn something every run. Blindly doing runs only tires you out.

Do full runs. Many racers ride short sections, rest a bit, scope out the course, and then continue. Not Peaty.

© Alan Davis

Curtis Keene, the fastest electrician in Fremont, California, attacks the aspens at the 2003 national downhill in Durango, Colorado.

Settle for Good Odds

The 2003 NORBA national downhill course at Purgatory Mountain Resort in Durango, Colorado, had one tricky rock section. Many racers, including pros, spent their entire practice sessions trying to devise routes through the slick, pointy, off-camber granite. Even Steve Peat was cleaning the section only four out of five tries. Rather than waste time worrying about it, he settled for his success rate and went for it in his race run. He knew everyone else was having the same trouble or worse, and if he did lose time he could make it up elsewhere on the course. In his race run, he got through the rocks perfectly and then, as he appeared at the bottom of the course, he overbaked an easy off-camber corner and crashed. He got back on his bike and still won handily. If you're only making a section one out of five times, you'd better find another way around.

Try not to get balled up in practice. Get through the section, learn what you can, and move on.

He rides top to bottom every time, and he emphasizes different sections on every run. When race time comes, he knows exactly how long he has to withstand the pummeling.

Practice fast.   Some racers start slow and get faster as they do more runs. This is a safe way to go, but things always change when you go faster in your race run. Peaty hauls the mail on every run. "People say my first practice run could be my qualifying run," he says. Peaty hits some sections faster in practice than he does in his race run. In a full-out race run, he might be too tired to pedal as much or hold on as well. But by hitting everything at full speed plus, he knows he and his bike are ready and nothing will catch him by surprise. "Some people say I should be more methodical," he says, "but this works for me."

Stay flexible.   Courses change. Roots and rocks break out and kick loose. Lines grow out of nowhere. Keep your eyes open and adjust your plan. Sometimes you have to adjust during your race run, so when you make your final race plan, leave room for interpretation.

Keep thinking.   Between runs, go over the course, your lines, and your speed. Which lines should I try this time? Where can I go faster? Compare notes with people you trust. Watch fast riders, but keep in mind that pros easily do things that would maim you.

"Sometimes it hurts to watch other people," says Peat. "It looks like they're hauling ass, and you get all worried, but if you watch yourself ride the section, you're hauling ass too. It's a big mind trip. You have to concentrate on your own thing."

Pay attention to people you respect. If Peat is at a 4X and he is watching or maybe gets eliminated early (youch!), when he tells me (Brian), "You got it," that assures me that I definitely have it. I kind of know already, but when I hear that, it really clicks.

Don't freak out on the tough sections.   Don't spend too much time working on any one section, be it a humongous jump, slippery rock garden, or whatever. Do what you can to get through the section, then move on. If you have time later, come back and get it dialed.

Imagine a race down the A-Line trail at the Whistler Mountain Bike Park. You haul the mail down this grooving trail, with berm after berm and dozens of perfect tabletop jumps. Then, all of a sudden, there's a big rock drop, with a wimp line that goes around it. A lot of guys would stand at that split all day watching other people and considering what to do, but if they just decide to skip the drop and lose two seconds, they can easily make up that time by learning the rest of the course.

Avoid the big hits.   In a race when your eyes pop out of your skull and your hands pump into useless claws, even a moderate hit can knock you out of whack. Besides, downhill bikes take enough of a beating without you bashing stuff willy-nilly. Says Peaty, "I run my bottom bracket low for better cornering, but I land on my MRP two or three times every run. If I hit things really hard in practice, I might break it in my race run, so I go smarter instead."

Do runs in your head. From your last practice to your race time, keep running through the course. Some racers even draw the course on paper. Relax and visualize yourself flowing down the course. Know you can do it, then go do it.

Prepare to pin it. "A downhill run isn't always fun," says Peaty, believe it or not. "There's a certain speed that's fun and flowy. You go beyond that."

Watch for Changing Lines

At the 2003 Durango national downhill, a nice left berm through the aspens got blown out in beginner/sport practice. Most pros missed the turn once before they adapted their lines, but Peaty saw the berm blowing out from the lift. He squared the turn as early as possible and carried speed over the roots into a long, straight section. If he had charged into the corner and stalled on the bad berm, it would have cost serious time.

Steve Peat squares off this turn before he falls into the blown-out berm from hell.

Sea Otter Classic Action With Lee

The 2003 Sea Otter Classic downhill course ended with over a minute of solid pedaling. I saved energy at the top of the course, passed a rider, and then hammered my brains out on the last flat section. As I approached the finish, pain filled my entire consciousness. About 30 feet out, I could barely turn the pedals. When I crossed the line I was completely done. I had budgeted my effort perfectly, and I wound up with a respectable second place.

Don't Go Too Hard

A two- to five-minute downhill run is smack dab in the "mystery zone" between your aerobic and anaerobic energy systems. You basically want to go as hard as you can without becoming stupid. When each of us gets over a certain heart rate, we lose focus and make mistakes. It's better to ride a bit too easy and clean than to ride too hard and sloppy. In a perfect run, lactic acid should build up in your muscles the whole way, so when you finally cross the line, you can barely hold on or pedal. There's a nice satisfaction in knowing you left nothing behind on the course. Practice at different intensities to learn where your line lies.

A downhill run is a series of short sprints and recoveries. Drop the hammer on flat sections and try to recover before you reach the technical sections. Decide where to pedal, where to pump, and where to rest. On steep descents, pedal up to speed and then coast. You waste a lot of energy pedaling against wind resistance.

Qualify Smart

At some races, you do a qualifying run before the final run. The faster you qualify, the later you race. If the course is likely to get rained on as the day progresses, try qualifying with a slow time so you can race earlier on a nice track. This is a bit risky, but every once in a while a nobody wins a big race because the honchos raced on a bad course.

The opposite applies as well: If it's going to get dryer as the day goes, you better pin it in qualifying.

Avoid Arm Pump

You know the feeling: You barrel down a rough course and your forearms start to ache. Pretty soon the aching becomes unbearable and you can barely hold onto your bars, much less control your bike.

Your forearm muscles are surrounded by a thin, inflexible sheath called a *fascia*. When you work those muscles hard, they swell up with blood and a painful pressure builds within the sheath. The higher the pressure gets, the more your veins get squished and the less blood can flow away from the muscles. Meanwhile, your arteries are squirting blood like a high-pressure fire hose, and even more blood gets trapped in the muscles. This further increases the pressure and pain and makes it even harder to ride your bike.

Some motocross racers, including ex–mountain bike downhill racer Shawn Palmer, have gotten their fascias cut open or removed to relieve this pressure. Don't worry: You can control the pump with less-invasive remedies. In order of importance:

Relax.   Your forearm muscles work best when you use them for a short time and then let them rest. Be sure to loosen your grip in the smooth sections, even if just for a second. In hectic situations it feels like a little demon is pulling on your forearm tendons, but you must concentrate on relaxing those muscles. You'll get less arm pump, plus you'll ride more smoothly.

Be in great shape.   The better your aerobic condition, the better your circulation. To prepare your hands for the stress of downhill racing, ride rough terrain a lot or ride motocross. If you can hang onto a moto, your DH bike will feel like a basket of flowers.

These exercises will give you Popeye forearms:

○   Wrist curls and extensions. With a barbell or light dumbbells, bust out three sets of 20 or more reps.

○   Dowel of death. Take a five-pound weight, tie it to a four-foot rope, and hang it from a wooden rod. Use both hands to turn the rod and wind the weight upward. Lower the weight slowly, then wind it back up in the opposite direction.

Practice These Skills

Downhill racing rewards exceptional strength and bike-handling skills. Here are some things to focus on.

Go fast.   If you want to race fast, you have to practice fast. "I ride fast all the time," says Peat. "It keeps your body and reflexes in tune. Anything to stay faster than the next guy." Of course, you should haul ass only in designated areas and never on public trails.

Get used to gnarl.   If you go to a race and encounter something—a huge jump, sticky mud, pointy rocks—and ask yourself, "Uh-oh, how am I going to do this?" you're going to end up slow, struggling, or crashed. The terrain on racecourses should never shock you; it should challenge you to go as fast as possible. Be sure to practice on the most extreme terrain you can handle, and pay special attention to the things that give you fits: off-camber turns, slippery roots, or whatever. When you get to your next race you should be saying to yourself, "Aw, this is easy. Now what's the fastest line?"

Pedal everywhere.   Practice cranking out of every turn and between every rough section. If you're not pedaling, you should be pumping.

Intensity.   Get used to spending two to five minutes going as hard as you can without losing control. You can do intervals on the road, but there's no substitute for fast runs on real terrain. Pedaling until your eyes bleed is step one; maintaining control while you're seeing red is step two. Downhillers need good aerobic fitness, but they don't need the mileage the XC guys need. A few hard, one-hour rides per week will do the trick.

Get Out of the Way!

"I would have let you by, but it would have cost me 5 or 10 seconds"—this from a racer who had been caught after a 60-second interval.

If you're in a downhill or other time-trial event and someone makes up 20, 30, or even 60 seconds and appears on your tail, don't try to speed up or block him. Get out of the way! Don't ruin someone else's winning run just to elevate yourself from 27th to 26th place.

If you're the one doing the catching, call out from way back so your fellow racer can find a good spot to let you by. When you do pass, do it all at once. There is a special hell for people who refuse to let faster racers pass. It's right down the hall from sandbagger hell.

Fuel Up

You don't need much fuel to get through a three-minute race. Just make sure you're hydrated and sharp. A Clif Shot 15 to 20 minutes before your run should give you the snap you crave.

Cross-Country

Cross-country racing, whether for 20 minutes, two hours, or an entire day, is just like normal cross-country riding, only it's faster, harder, and more painful. That and you ride in a tangle of type-A go-getters. And let's not forget the pain. Oh, the pain.

Cross-country racing demands a mix of strength, tactics, and toughness.

Hecka Tips

If you're into cross-country, you probably enjoy doing things the hard way. That's all well and good, but you might as well race smart.

Pace yourself.   Know your threshold and stay there. Push to the redline on the climbs and recover on the descents.

Respect your physical condition.   Do you feel well? Where are you in your training program? Don't shoot your wad if it's going to harm your future results or, worse, your health.

Know your competition.   Know which guys to go with in case they attack. If you're a better technical rider than a competitor, make sure you get to the single-track before him. If you're a great climber, don't take chances on the descents. Just get down safe and hammer on the way up.

Preride the course.   Know where to push and where to recover, when to hold 'em and when to fold 'em.

Use the feed zones.   Don't carry any more food or water than you need to. For short laps, pick up half-filled water bottles and maybe a shot of energy gel.

Pick the right bike.   Hardtails rule smooth courses. Dual suspension treats you right on rough courses. The longer and more brutal the course, the more likely you should run suspension.

Deal With Traffic

Unless you start like a nitro-burning funny car, you'll eventually have some characters in your way. And that means choking dust, annoying slowdowns, and possibly a poor result. To dominate the world of mass-start racing, you'd best learn to pass.

Warm up to start fast.   If the starting straight leads to a singletrack, you need to get there ahead of the sheep. Warm up thoroughly, line up near the front, and pin it to the singletrack. Once you're safely ahead of the flock, use your superior handling skills to recover—while still hauling.

Don't follow.   Think of other racers as obstacles, like trees. You wouldn't ride up to a tree, hit the brakes, and wait for the tree to move out of the way, would you? Most cross-country races end up being parades, with each racer sheepishly following a rear wheel. As long as you follow, you can't keep an eye out for passing spots, and you end up part of the flock. Baaa.

Pass smoothly.   Don't waste energy catching someone, slowing to the same speed, and then accelerating past. As you overtake another racer, plan your pass so you can whiz by without braking or accelerating. Try to pass in corners. Sorry to say this, but most recreational cross-country racers can't turn worth a damn; they slow down too much, take early apexes, and stall on the exit. Bust out a high–low or low–high pass, or blitz through a far-inside line. Remember: If it's within the course markings, it's legal. That narrow strip of tracked dirt is fine for slow sheep, but not for a speedy wolf like you. (Check out the passing section in this chapter, page 164.)

Roll like a freight train. If you must pass on a pedaling section, start accelerating from behind and zoom right by. If possible, slow your breathing, smile, and say something like, "Nice day!" or "When does the race start?" When your competitor is already on the brink of emotional collapse, this can be enough to make him trade his bike for a bass boat.

The World According to Weir

© Alan Davis

The mighty Mark Weir applies some hurt—to himself and others—at the 2004 Sea Otter Classic.

Mark Weir races professional downhill, singlespeed, cross-country, 24-hour races, and any other event that combines bikes and pain. He did the following interview with us in February, 2004.

In 2003, his team won the four-man open class at the 24-hour national championships, on single-speeds, with Weir riding the fastest lap overall. He broke the record at the 14.5-mile Downieville Downhill, despite a longer-than-ever course. The following weekend he took second overall in the Mt. Tamalpais road hill climb.

Weir handles a bike like a pro downhiller and makes power like a pro cross-country racer, but his passion for riding and his willingness— no, his desire—to suffer have made him the poster boy for soul-riding tough guys. Mr. Weir on what it takes to put the wood to your competition:

Chase Your Goals

When I ran a 45:54 at Mt. Tam in 2002, I set the goal of running a 42:00 the next year. I knew that would put me in the top three overall.

continued ➡

For a month and a half before the race, I would ride over the mountain to Stinson Beach and do a timed run up the course at 90 percent, then ride home. My total ride would be 70 miles and 7,500 feet of climbing. I did that three times a week. By the time the race came, I knew the course; it was all laid out in my head. When I caught the lead group, I didn't realize someone was out in front, and I didn't have time to catch him, so I got second with a 42:29. But that wasn't too bad considering the winner was a pro from the Navigator road team. (Glen Mitchell beat Weir by a mere 36 seconds.)

It's all about being focused. Take baby steps and accomplish your goals. That makes it fun and you get stuff done.

Become a Lean, Mean Fighting Machine

You want to be as light and skinny as possible. Like Lance says, be light and spin. In the off-season I'm 170 pounds and 7 percent body fat. When I race Downieville and Mt. Tam, I get down to 155 pounds.

I basically follow the no-food diet. Well, some food is involved. I eat only organic foods, whole grains, and lots of beans and pasta, and I live on organic peanut-butter sandwiches. I eat fish a couple times a week and I stay away from red meat; it makes me feel slow. I eat six times a day. It's basically snacking and always feeling hungry.

Two days before Downieville and Mt. Tam, I take a full-on colon cleaner. I go to Whole Foods Market and buy psyllium husk—the bottle with the large intestine on it so I know what I'm getting. It gives you the total vacuum treatment. I've lost four pounds in a dump.

Make Your Training Brutal But Fun

I look forward to winter. We ride our 35-pound freeride bikes with chain guides and 38-tooth rings. We put the seats low and we stand the entire time; it's our strength training. They say you should do six-hour rides on the road at 60 percent of your max. I do three to four hours at 80 percent on the mountain bike. We do rides with 5,000 feet of climbing, and we climb 25,000 feet in a week. I ride all over. I punish myself for five hours then ride home. It's what I like to do.

For a month and a half before my first race of the season, I spin the road bike for three to four hours a day. It's low intensity. It doesn't hurt you, especially after those five-hour mountain death rides. When I get on the road bike, I feel like a new man.

I've been racing for almost 10 years. In the beginning I did intervals and all that stuff. It stripped the life out of me. Ride the bike you have the most fun on. Listen to your body. If you're tired, back off and the next day you'll be full of fire.

If you aren't having fun, you can't go fast. My program might not create a national cross-country champion, but you never know—we'll see this year!

Obsess Over the Course

The Downieville course is like a slide show in my head. When you ride as much as I have, you can feel the way the trail flows across the mountain. You remember all the rocks that gave you a hard time. I see a snapshot in my head of a gray rock in the left corner that I have to turn around. Landmarks like this help you remember even the longest trails.

continued ➡

For months before the race, I lie in bed with a stopwatch and visualize the course. I have trouble sleeping. Maybe that's why. The course is 40 minutes long, and I always finish within 30 seconds of that. (Weir ran a 39:48 in real life.) If you focus and you're a complete psycho and you have no life but Downieville, you can win.

Pace Yourself, Sort Of

In local races I pin it until I drop everyone, especially the fast guys I want to punish.

The start is key. Even in a two- to three-hour race you have to pin it, especially at a national. I go as hard as I possibly can. At around 20 or 25 minutes, I want to quit. I can't believe the pain, and that I paid money for it. Then I start feeling better and find my rhythm. If I get passed in my rhythm, I have to let the rider go and hope to catch up later.

Maybe it's easier for the superhumans, I don't know. But that's what I have to do.

Embrace the Pain

Short-track races are 20 to 25 minutes, and they are the most painful thing you can do to your body. People say cyclocross is the worst, but I've done it and short track is worse. You can't find your rhythm and you almost soil yourself.

There's a big scale in your head. You're asking yourself, is it worth it? What outweighs what? You just gotta say "what the heck." You're not going to carcass like when you huck off a cliff. I'll just go as hard as I can and see what happens.

At the Sea Otter dirt criterium, Matt Gerken climbed so hard that he passed out on the descent. Dude, I want that gene that makes me go so hard that I don't care.

Embrace the Pain

Bike riding is hard. Bike riding at race pace is very hard. Sometimes it feels like the universe is made of pain and a funnel is pouring all of it onto your head.

Know your pain. Most of us think all pain is unpleasant, uncool, and worth avoiding. But there's a bad kind of pain—the kind you feel when you void your clavicle warranty—and a good kind of pain—the kind you feel when you push hard. Realize that the pain of effort is a good sign. It means you're pushing hard, getting stronger, and, hopefully, putting the hurt on someone.

If you feel terrible, take a moment to figure out why. Are you tense? Relax. Are you pedaling poorly? Smooth it out. Are you yanking on the bars? Let 'em be. Are you panting like a dying dog? Breathe slowly and deeply. Are you going as hard as you can? Sorry, that straight-up hurts. But at least you're getting stronger. Pain is a doorway between the rider you are and the rider you want to be.

Breathe. When you panic, your breathing gets fast and shallow. And when your breathing gets fast and shallow, you tend to panic. It's a two-way feedback situation. So when you're panting and apprehensive like a Chihuahua, take it slow and deep like Jacques Cousteau. That should mellow you right out. Focus on slow, deep breaths down in your diaphragm.

Brian's Approach to Training

I don't follow any specific plan. I just ride, ride, ride. The kind of riding I do depends on what I'm preparing for. In general, I do lots of cross-country, BMX starts, jumping, and some road riding to make sure I have good all-around fitness. As the season approaches, I do more sprinting and less distance. I go by how I feel and I never use a heart-rate monitor.

During the off-season I lift weights about four days a week, concentrating on a different body part each day. I do high reps with low weight (low for him, not for the rest of us! —Lee). As the season begins, I stop lifting and concentrate on bike speed. All of the traveling I do makes me miss workouts, and I get too sore after a week off.

I love riding motocross. You can do everything on a moto that you can do on a bike, only twice as fast, twice as far, and twice as high. It gives you a full-body workout, and it get you used to going really fast over crazy terrain. I actually have a motocross track in my backyard. Heck, if I could make a living as a motocross racer, I'd do it in a second.

I also like to declare "Special Olympics" once in a while. We'll be hanging out at someone's house and I'll say, "Let's see who can jump up the most steps" or whatever. Competition is a way of life for me, and I'm always ready to go.

Brian "trains" on a BBR-prepped Honda CRF150 at an indoor track near Seattle.

Relax. If a muscle isn't directly carrying you up the hill, it should be slack. Make your hands, arms, and shoulders as limp as possible. When we get uncomfortable, we unconsciously contort our faces like gargoyles. Relax your jaw, your cheeks, and your eyes, and the rest of your body will follow.

Consult your HRM. A heart-rate monitor is a tachometer for your body. If you feel like you're going to die but your heart is in the green zone, then something else is going wrong. You might be tired, sick, dehydrated, or mired in terrible form. If you think you might be able to go harder and your HRM shows a safe reading, then go for it. If you're at redline, then it's a matter of maintaining the pace and dealing with the pain.

Think about something else. The more you focus on your pain, the more it fills your entire consciousness. If you focus on something else—anything—your pain will fade to the background. Perfect your stroke. Sing a song. Remember that everyone else is hurting just as much. If you can put your discomfort on the back shelf and get your competitors to concentrate on their agony, you can break them.

You can get through this. One of the biggest milestones in a new rider's life is when you realize you can bust a gut to clear a rise, and then recover and feel fine afterward. If you're in good shape, the pain is temporary.

Pace yourself. When you reach a long climb, start relatively easy, find a rhythm, and push harder as you reach the top. Upshift and keep pushing until you start to coast downhill. Recover on the way down. The buffoons who blasted from the bottom will hit their walls partway up, and there won't be any rest for them.

Remember, this is supposed to be fun. Right? Ha!

Fuel for Cross-Country Racing

Know your body. Know how long you can hammer without food. Try different drinks, gels, and solid foods on your training rides, especially those that mimic your race distance. We've seen guys consume pork chops and sardines on group rides. Gnarly. But, hey, do what works for you.

Shoot Your Troubles

Problem: Fellow racers accuse you of sandbagging.

Solution: Thank this book for making you faster—and then upgrade to a higher class!

Competition adds challenge, excitement, and validation to an already-cool sport. If you've never raced before, we suggest you pick an event that appeals to you. Race locally against your buddies or travel to a new place. Go in with an open attitude and reasonable expectations, and you'll have a great time. If you're already a serious racer, keep training, baby! We'll bet this book helps make you even faster.

How Good Is Your Kung Fu?

When you master every skill in this list, you will be one heck of a good all-around mountain biker. For each move, give yourself two points if you rule the roost, one point if you get by, and zero points if you don't even know what we're talking about.

____ You center your weight on the bike.

____ You mount and dismount like a Belgian cyclocross god.

____ When it comes to bailing out, you know when to hold 'em and when to fold 'em.

____ When you do crash, you do it with style—and all of your teeth.

____ You pedal smooth circles, not jerky rhombuses.

____ You can spin along at more than 90 rpm.

____ You can sprint beyond 120 rpm.

____ When it comes to slowing down, you haven't skidded since the first grade.

____ You realize braking bumps are for catching air, not braking.

____ You never commit to corners (or life partners) before you can see all the way through them.

____ When it gets gnarly, you point your fingers where you want to go. No panic braking.

____ Your bike bounces all over the place, but your head floats down the trail.

____ You corner so well, you practically come out faster than you went in.

____ You lean so far in berms, you can see under your tires.

____ Switchbacks seem wide and boring.

____ You're prepared to skid through a corner, but only if someone starts trouble first.

continued ➡

____ You see berms as sideways holes, to pump into and pop out of.

____ When your tires start to drift, you feel like you're finally getting somewhere.

____ You can pop a wheelie.

____ You can ride a wheelie.

____ You can manual on flat ground.

____ You can manual over a double.

____ You can hop over curbs.

____ You can bound over one-foot logs.

____ You can lunge onto a two-foot ledge.

____ If a coyote charges at your rear wheel, you can knock him senseless with a kickout.

____ On a double dare, you can pedal-hop from the sidewalk to the handrail overlooking Hoover Dam.

____ You can huck off a 10-foot drop and land on flat ground with nary a chain slap.

____ When you drop off an outcropping on a fast downhill, you get back to the car thinking you're still in the air, that's how smoothly you land.

____ Small tabletops are child's play.

____ You jump small doubles all day.

____ On big doubles, you go all the way.

____ You can boost a lip 'til you see your house.

____ You can stay so low you're below the mouse.

____ You pump a rhythm section as if there's a cheese reward at the end.

____ Hips aren't just for jeans; they're for jumping.

____ Transfers aren't for buses; they're for jumping too.

____ Jump into a turn? No problem.

____ You lay your bike so flat in the air, you could have a tea party up there.

____ You turn down your bike even more gracefully than you turn down the hotties.

____ Turn a bump into a jump without taking a lump.

____ When you need to haul the ass, you suck up a jump fully on the gas.

____ You have the Terminator's eyes; always scanning, always planning.

____ You pick the lines that your speed, bike, and skills define.

____ You know when to use speed, but you're too wise for momentum greed.

____ You use your brain, pump terrain, and ride with the grain.

____ You float over rough stuff.

____ You stay in control in the slick.

____ You stay on top of loose action.

____ You stay out of rain ruts unless they're also berms.

____ You ride the skinny like no ninny.

____ You have a good attitude in your riding and racing.

____ When the time comes, you get right into the racing zone.

____ You holeshot most of your bikercross/BMX races.

____ Slower riders are like trees you pass with ease.

____ You're hard to pass up.

____ You learn new courses quickly and effectively.

____ You know how to pace for any length race.

____ The only arm pump you get is in the gym.

____ Pain. Who cares, as long as you're getting strong?

YOUR TOTAL

____ 101-120—You are a true master.

____ 81-100—Your kung fu is good, but not good enough!

____ 61-80—Admirable. You have the makings of a fine student.

____ 0-60—You have lots of work to do. Wax on, wax off, Daniel-san.

Note: Brian scores a perfect 120. Lee gives himself a 95.

Great Riders in Great Places

Here's a guide to the riders pictured in this book and the fun locations they showed us their kung fu.

Page number	Rider	Location
i	Brian Lopes	Brian's backyard
iv	Brandon Sloan	Bootleg Canyon Mountain Bike Park, Boulder City, Nevada
1	Brian Lopes	Original Sin, Whistler Mountain Bike Park, British Columbia
17	Curtis Keene	Stanford Subatomic Smash Downhill, Santa Teresa County Park, San Jose, California
21 (top left)	Brian Lopes	A River Runs Through It, Whistler, British Columbia
21 (middle)	Brian Lopes	A River Runs Through It, Whistler, British Columbia
21 (bottom right)	Brandon Sloan	Bootleg Canyon Mountain Bike Park, Boulder City, Nevada
22	Brian Lopes	The Manager, Whistler Mountain Bike Park
23	Zach Griffith	Keystone Resort, Colorado
24 (left)	John Watt	Sourdough Trail near Ward, Colorado
24 (right)	Bobbi Kae Watt	The Fix jumps, Boulder, Colorado
25	Lee McCormack	Lake Arbor Jumps, Arvada, Colorado
27	Lee McCormack	
28	Lee McCormack	
31	Brian Lopes	A River Runs Through It, Whistler, British Columbia
34 and 35	Gunn-Rita Dahle	On a trainer in a friend's house, Boulder, Colorado
37	Brian Lopes	Eaton Park jumps, Gunbarrel, Colorado
38 (left)	Brian Lopes	A River Runs Through It, Whistler, British Columbia
38 (right)	Lee McCormack	White Ranch, Golden, Colorado

Page number	Rider	Location
39	Brian Lopes	Crankworx Freeride Mountain Bike Festival bikercross, Whistler Mountain Bike Park
45	Zach Griffith	Keystone Resort, Colorado
49 (top)	Marla Streb	2003 national downhill course, Durango, Colorado
53	Bobbi Kae Watt	Arvada BMX Track, Arvada, Colorado
56	Cameron Zink	2004 national downhill course, Big Bear Lake, California
57	Lee McCormack	A handy baseball diamond, Boulder, Colorado
60	Brian Lopes	Dacono BMX Track, Dacono, Colorado
61 (left)	Brian Lopes	Dirt Merchant, Whistler Mountain Bike Park
61 (right)	Lee McCormack	The Shells, Redwood City, California
63	Greg Minnaar	2004 national downhill course, Big Bear Lake, California
64	Brian Lopes	Brian's backyard
65	Brian Lopes	Dirt Merchant, Whistler Mountain Bike Park
66	Jon Watt	Secret training grounds
67	Steve Peat	2004 national downhill course, Big Bear Lake, California
68	Zach Griffith	Keystone Resort, Colorado
69	Steve Peat	2004 national downhill course, Big Bear Lake, California
70	Brian Lopes	Secret training grounds
75	Brian Lopes	A River Runs Through It, Whistler, British Columbia
77	Curtis Keene	
78	Curtis Keene	
79 (top)	Curtis Keene	
79 (bottom)	Lisa Myklak	The Fix jumps, Boulder, Colorado
80 (top)	Brian Lopes	Hall Ranch, Lyons, Colorado
80 (bottom)	Curtis Keene	
81	Lee McCormack	In front of Lee's house
82	Curtis Keene	
83	Curtis Keene	
85	Brian Lopes	Whistler Mountain Bike Park skills center
86	Lee McCormack	White Ranch, Golden, Colorado

Page number	Rider	Location
87	Brian Lopes	
89	Unknown	A-Line, Whistler Mountain Bike Park
92	Brian Lopes	Whistler Mountain Bike Park
93	Brian Lopes	Whistler Mountain Bike Park skills center
94	Brian Lopes	Clown Shoes, Whistler Mountain Bike Park
95	Brian Lopes	Whistler Mountain Bike Park skate park
97	Brian Lopes	Joyride 4X course, Kamloops, British Columbia
99	Bobbi Kae Watt	The Fix jumps, Boulder, Colorado
100	Brian Lopes	Whistler Mountain Bike Park dirt jumps
101	Brian Lopes	Whistler Mountain Bike Park dirt jumps
102	Brian Lopes	Whistler Mountain Bike Park dirt jumps
103	Brian Lopes	Whistler Mountain Bike Park dirt jumps
105 (left)	Matt Vujicevich	Calabasas Jump Park, San Jose, California
105 (right)	Curtis Keene	Calabasas Jump Park, San Jose, California
106 and 107	Brian Lopes	Dacono BMX Track, Dacono, Colorado
109	Brian Lopes	Brian's backyard
110	Matt Vujicevich	Crabapple Hits, Whistler Mountain Bike Park
111	Matt Vujicevich	Boneyard Slopestyle Park, Whistler Mountain Bike Park
112	Curtis Keene	The Shells, Redwood City, California
113	Brian Lopes	Whistler Mountain Bike Park dirt jumps
114 (top)	Brian Lopes	Dacono BMX Track, Dacono, Colorado
114 (bottom)	Matt Vujicevich	Boneyard Slopestyle Park, Whistler Mountain Bike Park
115	Brian Lopes	Whistler Mountain Bike Park dirt jumps
116	Steve Wentaz	Secret training grounds
117	Brian Lopes	Lake Arbor jumps, Arvada, Colorado
118	Brian Lopes	Eaton Park jumps, Gunbarrel, Colorado
119	Brian Lopes	Hall Ranch, Lyons, Colorado
120	Brian Lopes	Whistler Mountain Bike Park jumps
123	Brian Lopes	Original Sin, Whistler Mountain Bike Park
126		2003 national downhill course, Durango, Colorado
129	Zach Griffith	Keystone Resort, Colorado

Index

About the Authors

© Josh McGuckin

Authors Lee McCormack (left) and Brian Lopes (right).

Brian Lopes has been a prevailing force on the professional mountain biking scene for more than a decade and is now recognized as the winningest professional mountain bike racer in the United States. He has earned nine National Off-Road Bicycle Association (NORBA) Championships, four World Cup Championships, and two World Championships.

Lopes started riding at age 4 and graduated to pro status at 17. Since then, he has dominated BMX, downhill, dual slalom, dual, and most recently bikercross racing. He is the most successful active racer on the NORBA circuit, regardless of discipline, and has held world records in bunny hopping and distance jumping. Lopes has appeared on the Outdoor Life Network, has graced the covers of every major mountain biking magazine, including *Bike, Dirt, Bicycling, VeloNews,* and *Mountain Biking*, and has received coverage in such mainstream media as *Men's Health, Rolling Stone,* and *USA Today*.

Featured in numerous riding videos, Lopes even has a signature tire—the Maxxis Brian Lopes Bling Bling Dual. He also stars in the mountain bike video game *Downhill Domination* for PlayStation. Other career highlights include being nominated as ESPY's Extreme Athlete of the Year and serving as a stunt rider for the USA Network show *Pacific Blue*.

Lopes resides in Trabuco Canyon, California, with his wife, Paula.

Lee McCormack is an experienced journalist who has written for *Bike, Mountain Bike Action*, *Twentysix, Flow,* and *Mountain Biking.* He also publishes www.leelikesbikes.com, a mountain biking Web site frequented by thousands of readers worldwide.

McCormack has won numerous writing and informational graphics awards at the state and regional levels and was part of the team that won the 1998 Pulitzer Prize for public service. He enjoys all riding disciplines from singletrack to road to dirt jumps. McCormack has been an expert-level downhill and slalom racer for several years, and his riding has dramatically improved since working with Lopes on this book. In 2004 McCormack won several major events and finished the year ranked No. 1 among expert downhillers within his age class. He is now positioned to turn semipro in 2005.

McCormack lives in Boulder, Colorado, with his wife, Tracy.

Excel

in your next endurance challenge

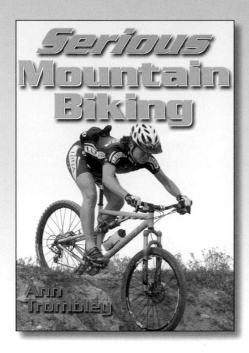

Ride faster and smarter than ever before!

Olympian, former national champion, and elite cycling coach Ann Trombley is your expert guide in *Serious Mountain Biking*. Get answers to the questions and solutions to the problems you've encountered while participating in the sport, including information on

- selection and fitting of equipment for the optimal match of personal attributes with current technology,
- technical maneuvers that maximize both speed and safety,
- training methods and workouts that yield superior results, and
- racing preparations and tactics that make competition more rewarding and more successful.

Make every minute and mile you invest on the bike more beneficial and enjoyable with the help of this invaluable resource!

240 pages • ISBN 0-7360-5499-5

Improve your race strategies and skills!

Adventure Racing is your complete guide to the skills, equipment, strategies, navigation, and nutrition used by the top adventure racers around the globe. Learn the skills for trekking, mountain biking, canoeing, kayaking, and mountaineering, including information on

- the right gear to perform your best—even in desert, rainforest, and subzero environments,
- team strategy, use of support crews, map reading, and magnetic deviation to keep you on track, and
- the right fuel for changing conditions, medical know-how, and survival skills to keep you in the race.

Profiles and stories from top races and adventure racers will provide a taste of the exciting challenges of the sport, inspiring you to test yourself time and again in the most addictive team endurance sport on the planet!

160 pages • ISBN 0-7360-5911-3

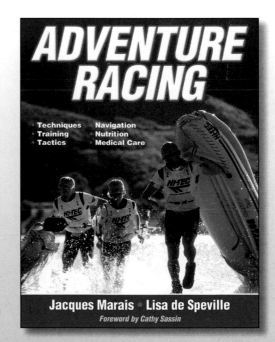